My way with jiu-jitsu

From beginner to black belt

Master Horst D. Lindenau

"Make sure you continue with your training after receiving 1st Dan black belt"

About the book

This valuable book is the result of what we call work sheets at our local school Ichinen Bridport/UK. For many years the author has published these work sheets and handed them out to hundreds of students. The basics and the most important information about our way with Jiu-Jitsu are now concentrated in this little compendium. It shall support the practitioner from the very start and encourage every student to proceed on their way to become a black belt one day and keep this precious martial art alive and pass it on to further generations.

Master Horst D. Lindenau

About the author

Master Horst D. Lindenau started Jiu-Jitsu training 1987 in Germany. His background is from Judo and Shotokan Karate and he found his perfect martial art style in the traditional Japanese way of Jiu-Jitsu. After 33 years of training and studying Jiu-Jitsu he is a 2nd Dan black belt today.

The author is a 6th Dan Grand master in the international style of BlackCombat, which is the successor of Anti Terror Combat and was renamed in 2018. Additionally he is a bearer of several more black belts in various styles and has taught 1000's of students worldwide. Master Horst is a well known blogger in the martial arts world and publishes his knowledge in print as well as with the new media online. The online presence of his own school Ichinen Bridport is www.ichinenbridport.com

He has traveled all over the world, visited 68 countries so far and lived and worked in seven countries for over a year and studied the martial arts there. This includes Japan and the USA. Currently Master Horst lives in the southwest of England. "The grass is greener where you water it." (Wise words by Master Horst)

My way with Jiu-Jitsu

From beginner to black belt

A detailed instruction on the road to your first black belt.

This personal journey encourages and supports you to go your way.

Includes the full syllabus from white belt to the black belt as used at Ichinen Bridport.

Illustrated with drawings and photos from the author.

Photo front cover: Master Horst D. Lindenau congratulates his friend Trevor Barton † for his 3rd Kyu Jiu-Jitsu in February 2017

Published by Amazon Books

1st edition published May 2019

2nd edition published August 2019

Disclaimer

Although both Ichinen Bridport and the author of this pamphlet have taken great care to ensure the authenticity of the information and techniques published herein, we are not responsible, in whole or in part, for any injury which may occur to the reader by following any instructions given in this book. We also do not guarantee that the techniques described within here will be safe and effective in a self defence situation. It is understood that there is a potential for injury when using or demonstrating the techniques herein described. It is essential that the reader who follows any of the described techniques should seek medical advice to ensure he/she is fit to do so and understands the risk of a possible injury. Also, national and local law may prohibit the use or possession of weapons described herein.

Information and recommendations presented in this book are based on training, own personal experience and extensive research. Application of the recommendations and information given in this book are undertaken at the individuals own risk. All recommendations and information given here are without any guarantee on the part of the author or publisher, their agents or employees. Of necessity, the author and publisher disclaim all liability in connection with the use of information presented herein, which should always be used on a basis of a gift – sound common sense.

Note: Throughout the book individuals are referred to as "he". This should, of course, be taken to mean "he" or "she" or "any other" where appropriate.

1st edition 5.2019

Content

DEDICATION

To the one anywhere in the world who wants to pick up any martial art. This compilation is the result of working with my awesome students for over 30 years. And to my masters who taught me before and now and which I am very thankful about. My Grand master once said to me "in the student you recognize the master" and I truly can say, I have learned this fine martial art of Jiu-Jitsu by walking the path with my students. Thank you all!

ACKNOWLEDGMENTS

I wish to express my deep and lasting appreciation to my friends and associates who have assisted me in the preparation of this book. Special thanks to Ruth Hennigan and Master Lewis A. Harris for their big help to edit some of the written parts of the book. And special thanks to my friends and students Kieren, Alfie, Sascha, Finlay, Fred and Dillon for given me the permission to use their photographs. And special thanks to all the masters and teachers worldwide who taught me their skills and to the students I trained with and those I taught. You are all part of this book.

Foreword

Your body is the boat with which you sail through life. Therefore it is only natural that this boat, your body, is in an immaculate condition. You want to be physically, mentally, emotionally and spiritually well and of good health. And you want to feel safe and positive. Then the ancient martial art of Jiu-Jitsu is the right choice for you. The Jiu-Jitsu described in this book has its origins in the ancient history of Japan. It comes today in many variations and you might find it as Ju Jutsu or Ju Jitsu or any other writing. Here we use Jiu-Jitsu, which is probably the best translation from Japanese for us Westerners.

Winning by losing

Winning by losing, or the soft art, is the nearest translation and that describes it pretty accurately. The Jiu-Jitsu from its historic roots can be called "the mother of all martial arts" if we look at the Japanese influence. From this beginning many other well known disciplines have been developed from Jiu-Jitsu, such as Karate, Aikido or Judo.

This book is your guidance

Of course they all have their own rights and whenever we talk about any other styles the rule is:

"The Mountain does not criticise the river for not being as high and the river does not criticise the mountain for not having any water."

"Where there is no style, there is no slave." (Wise words by Master Horst)

And as you progress with your Jiu-Jitsu stay always open to other styles and don't just confine yourself to only one school. Continue your training, your progress, your studies of the martial arts. When you want to sail through life and use this Jiu-Jitsu to build and protect your boat, to master all the unknown waters and sail through many "hurricanes", then you will find all that you need to begin your own journey, in this book.

From the beginning to black belt standard it is a personal journey for you, as it was for me and "**My way with Jiu-Jitsu**" shall give you a little help to be successful on your own way. We will look together at the history and background of this grand system and a practical section of the various grading levels gives you a help to reach your goal step by step. Self defence and the law, self motivation and physical health issues will be discussed by looking at the anatomy of the human body, government guidelines and spiritual exercises. But without you entering the dojo on a regular basis, it will just remain a dream.

This book is written to sum up the content of the work sheets I have passed on to my students over the years. It is my true conviction that one of the most useful things I have done in my life is to practice this art of Jiu-Jitsu. Hopefully you will get a spark of it and follow me with your boat on this exciting voyage.

And this book, I should finally say, is not designed to be read for sound bites. That is the reason why it does not have an index. It should be read ideally as a love story, like a novel, which describes in detail the beautiful and compelling love relationship between Jiu-Jitsu and the practitioner.

Why train Jiu-Jitsu?

Or why train any martial art in the first place?

Many connect martial arts first with the element of self defence in it. But I would like to show you that there is much more.

Think about the mental aspect of the art. Physical activity, repetition is used to perfect a certain move. Hundreds, in some cases thousands of executions are needed until the proper technique can be achieved. This is only possible if the focus is maintained at all times and mind and body work together as a unit.

Another very important aspect of any martial arts training are postures and stances. Even before kicking and punching, one must learn the correct body alignment and center of gravity placement.

A good balance is needed for execution of any techniques. Balance is a key factor to all movements, regardless of its nature. Lack of balance diminishes the work that was already done to master any move.

In Jiu-Jitsu the kicks are not predominant but still in most levels required. Therefore it is necessary to develop a good flexibility and do your stretching. It is compulsory to have a good level of power, strength and fitness to train Jiu-Jitsu. This is not only important for your own health, but needed in competitions as in self defence.

A brief introduction into Jiu-Jitsu

A few days ago I read a book on Jiu-Jitsu and some guy said "what you read here is the future of Jiu-Jitsu". Sounds to me like years ago the German section of Wing-Chun claimed their style is the most effective in fighting. To keep that clear, there is NO best style and there is no one who can predict the future. It always has to do with people who want to make a business from their martial art. Let them do. This way too is part and a way of martial arts and how it went through the centuries. It all belongs together and works together.

Here at Ichinen Bridport (www.ichinenbridort.com) our Jiu-Jitsu is traditional. The aim is to train ourselves for personal growth and up to a good standard of self defence. And as we go along this long path of teaching and learning, we find out, the biggest enemy lies inside our self.

Why is that traditional? Well, as far as we know, Jiu-Jitsu was mentioned first in ancient Japan. It was then purely a method of fighting, against unarmed and armed attackers. And today nothing has changed. Only the objects one might be attacked with are different.

There is only a little known from ancient history of Jiu-Jitsu. Not only because it is some time ago, when it was first practiced and mentioned as such a style, but as it is originated from Japan, there are just too little translations and reports available in the West. In Japan it was wide spread among the different schools and styles to keep the teachings secret.

Jiu-Jitsu can be traced back to the 16th century and some 150 years ago there been over 1000 different schools in Japan. All practicing their very own style.

13

If we look at the techniques we use, a lot of them are found in many other martial art styles. But this is only because a human being has got two arms and two legs. A punch is a punch and a throw is a throw. Names are not important; it is rather the question if I can do it and is it effective when I need it?

"Speed – Technique - Power." (Wise words by Master Horst)

If there wouldn't be a restriction today, who and what is legal to teach, I probably just would call it "Bridport Self Defence" by Master Horst. But one needs an insurance for training and teaching nowadays and need to join some kind of authorized body to gain that. The techniques would be the same. What is useful for self defence is found in our syllabus.

It is your choice to start at your local Jiu-Jitsu club or travel a bit further to the next town. In our case, here in the little town of Bridport in the Southwest of England, we are the only school in reach which teaches Jiu-Jitsu. Make your own decision by finding upfront information about your local club and go and have a trial session. It is very often a choice of the instructor you find and if there are friendly and welcoming students for the beginner to join with.

If Jiu-Jitsu, Ju Jutsu, Jujitsu or just Jutsu, these are only names, translated by someone and again the names vary in different countries. In Germany, Jiu-Jitsu is connected to sport competitions, the more newish Brazilian Jiu-Jitsu which is found internationally, is concentrating mostly on wrestling like techniques as our style here at Ichinen Bridport has the aim of purely self defence and mental and physical stability.

The nearest translation for Jiu-Jitsu I assume is "winning by losing" or "the soft art". We are told by various authorities that it originated in China and/or India. Further developed in Japan in the ancient time of the Samurais… From that Jiu-Jitsu many other martial arts were born. Just mention Karate, Judo or Aikido.

This is the Japanese "Kanji" which stands for soft, gentle, flexible

This is the Japanese "Kanji" which stands for art and execution

Both together gives us the Jiu-Jitsu symbol as we know it in the West.

Today Jiu-Jitsu is a really fine all-round martial art, developing a well proportioned and supple body. You learn self control and mental and physical relaxation. Jiu-Jitsu calls for courage and endurance. And above all, it develops patience, perseverance and consideration for other people. You will learn to be cooperative and gain a sense of respect, honor as well as self confidence.

At Ichinen Bridport Jiu-Jitsu school we learn this art to defend ourselves against one or several, unarmed or armed attacker. We train in the Dojo on comfy mats and sometimes we move our training to the outdoors too. The repertoire of our syllabus includes not only the traditional techniques like throws, arm bars, head locks, transport grips and strangling, holds on the ground etc., but also pulling someone hair, even spitting and biting can be found. All striking, kicking, punching is included.

And of course, the training involves all legal natural weapons found in this country. Where they are illegal we use replicas. On top of that we train with all kind of unnatural weapons.

For most of our techniques we use Japanese names. This is often simpler than trying to find a useful translation or come up with your own brand, but it reflects mainly our traditional Japanese style. That means you will learn a fair amount of Japanese terms too. And using these terms helps us maintain tangible links to our heritage.

Jiu-Jitsu taken in steps

General information about grading from white belt to black belt

All martial arts organizations and institutions use a grade-levelling system that helps differentiate between positions, recognition and skills available by an individual member.

Imagine a company which employs technicians, support specialists, sales persons, marketing and human resource managers and so on. It would be challenging to ensure consistent and fair compensation across these many different roles without creating some form of standard mechanism. Fact is that for every position, there are varying levels, including junior or senior roles. The grade level system in Jiu-Jitsu does just that.

"You must be willing to invest your time towards the goal." (Wise words by Master Horst)

Judo belts are considered to be the originator of the belt systems we have in most martial arts today. Judo belts didn't have the wide variety of colours as we see today. There was only a white and a brown belt as student grade before the black belt in the past. The founder of Judo, Jigoro Kano started a formal ranking procedure around 1883 when he awarded two of his students the rank of Shodan which is the lowest black belt rank.

Even then this was not externally visible. He had not invented the modern Judo Gi or belt yet. No one could tell from looking at clothing what grade people were as they all wore the same clothes, which at this time was a white kimono. In 1886 Kano was said to have made his Dan grades with the belts on their kimonos as the first visual sign of a grade. And only in 1907 Kano invented the modern Judo Gi and the Judo belt system.

Today we have a huge variety in not only styles but grades all over the world. The Americans picked up Kanos idea and introduced a fan of belts and different colours. Some add stripes to each colour belt to have even more variety.

One martial artist in Italy is said to have the 36th Dan in one single style. Well, each to their own. Where I live, just over the road is a Taekwondo club, they have a 12 year old girl who is a 2nd Dan. Some others do travel far abroad, mostly exotic destinations, only to come back with what rank ever. Even people do a cruise to do so nowadays. And so on it goes, which is not the subject of this book. Legally there is no system which regulates any of the grades.

In my Jiu-Jitsu style we start as student with a white belt, which comes with the Gi and adds a red stripe to it after the first grading. Followed by five coloured student belts and ten master grades. There are different rules for minors, but same belts colours.

The actual grading syllabus we use nowadays in our martial art school will give you a good idea what the different grades are made of.

We begin with the first grading for the 6th Kyu (white belt with a red stripe), which most students take after 3 – 4 months regular training.

The coloured belts of Jiu-Jitsu are called Obi

There are six student grades. They are called Kyu grades and count from 6th to 1st Kyu. After these student grades follow the master grades. They are called Dan grades and count from 1st to 10th Dan. My late Grandmaster used to say "I don't want the 10th Dan degree. They all die!" The usual time to gain the first black belt would be about three years of training for the amateur. This requires a more or less regular weekly training. The one who takes it more seriously and trains significantly more, could shorten this time if the knowledge and quality of performance is satisfying.

The syllabus is a requirement of rolls and falls, the techniques and as well physical and mental fitness, a theory section and an active role within the school to support it. All grading can be done within our school. For a Master/Dan grading three other Masters must be in the grading commission, where one of them must have a higher grade, than the graduate is aiming for. Student grades can be reviewed by one Dan grade, although in most cases the 1st Kyu grading is assisted by another high Kyu grade or even another Master. All this guaranties a good quality of each grade and certificate issued at our school.

The rolls and falls as well as the various techniques have to be shown as required according to the grade. The physical fitness is monitored by a regular fittest within the school and consists of pushups, sit ups and the leg split. The mental fitness is judged by the teacher. Regarding the school support I like to say, this is a little bit unique and to my knowledge only requested within Ichinen Bridport. We expect that any member actively supports the school. This can be through the use of social media, helping out at club events, help with recruiting new students and just simply spreading the word. Ichinen Bridport is supposed to be a school for all the members. Not just some institution where you pay a monthly fee and use it.

The grading syllabus in detail

The following content is today's temporary guideline for Jiu-Jitsu grading at Ichinen Bridport for the adult rank. It will always be progressive and change towards the needs and it can be altered to suit certain age levels or students with certain handicaps. For the under age, basically up to 16 years there is a different volume, which is not part of this book. You can suppose that the requirements are different in this case. It increases with the knowledge of the child and the progress towards black belt level.

It always raises the question of whether you should train the left and right side at the same time. I was trained myself firstly hand the right side techniques and I must admit, it served me well in competitions and in self defence situations. Studies show for example that in Germany there are about 90% right-handers. And the vast majority of people are right-footed people.

At Ichinen Bridport I teach all Jiu-Jitsu techniques right-handed. Exceptions are punches and kicks, elbow strikes and so on and the rolls and falls have to be mastered both sides after the yellow belt. And we leave it with every individual to decide which side they want to train.

All grades involve the rolls and falls. For the white belt with the red stripe, the 6th Kyu, these have to be done only one sided. After that left and right becomes compulsory. The rolls and falls are some kind of special and unique part of the syllabus.

Not only do we need these skills in an eventual fight, but these rolls and falls will make us really supple, capable and fit to cope with the rest of the skills. They are an excellent warming up exercise and train the motor activity.

"There is no physical technique without right mental performance." (Wise words by Master Horst)

6th Kyu/White belt-red stripe

Break falls: Roll forward, backward roll, fall sideways and fall backwards

1 throw

1 defence against strangle hold

1 strangling hold

1 hold down

1 wrist lock liberation

1 wrist lock

Ear nerve press

1 kick

1 arm lock

2 punch techniques

Theory:

What is Jiu-Jitsu? Why do I study Jiu-Jitsu? Jiu-Jitsu grading system, self defence and the law, Dojo etiquette.

This is the beginner's first step into the martial art Jiu-Jitsu. At Ichinen Bridport we teach the art not for sport to take part in championships, but purely for self defence and well being, self discipline and individual growth. Although if someone wants to fight competitions, he or she could do so and we support it.

 Training required is 3 months or 25 hours.

Student needs to support actively Ichinen Bridport

5th Kyu/Yellow belt

Break falls: Roll forward, backward roll, roll sideways, all left and right, fall forward, backward and sideways and 1 roll over an obstacle.

2 throws

2 strangling holds

1 defence against strangle hold

Ear nerve press

1 hold down

2 wrist locks

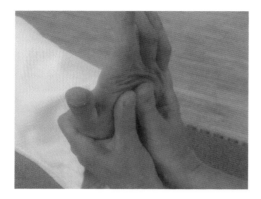

1 wrist lock liberation

Side kick / defence against knife attack

Throat nerve press, control attacker

This is my favorite self defence move and every student should master it. It is a very effective self defence technique and easy to learn.

2 arm locks

Theory:
Judo, Jiu-Jitsu, Kung Fu, Jiu-Jitsu grading system, self defence and the law, Japanese terms, Dojo etiquette, first aid.

Student needs to support actively Ichinen Bridport

Training required is 3 months or 25 hours from white belt grading

4th Kyu/Orange belt

Break falls
roll forward, backward roll, roll sideways, all left and right
fall forward, -back and sideways and 2 rolls over an obstacle

3 throws

3 strangling holds

2 hold downs and 1 liberation

2 transport grips

Throat nerve press, control attacker

2 arm locks

3 Karate techniques

3 Boxing techniques

Demonstrate one defence against the following situations:

1. 1. One person pushes, hands to chest, followed by the pusher striking to   the head.

2. A swinging punch to the head.

3. A front clothing grab, one handed, followed by a punch to the head / or a head butt

4. A front clothing grab, two hands, followed by the knee to the groin.

5. A bottle or glass to the head.

6. A lashing kick to the groin

7. A slash with knife

Theory:

-Judo = Japanese originated Budo system (Sport and personal education)

-Jiu-Jitsu = "the soft art", "winning by losing", an all-round martial art fighting system. Jiu-Jitsu is excellent for self defence.

-Karate = Japanese originated Budo system. Mainly involving hand and feet techniques, called "empty hand".

- Jiu-Jitsu grading system = white, yellow, orange, green, blue, brown, black. Use of natural and unnatural weapons

-Self defence and the law

-Japanese terms = Hajime: fight, start! / Yame: End, stop / Sensei: Master, teacher / Tatami: Mats / Gi: uniform / Obi: belt / Dojo: training hall

-Dojo etiquette

-First aid basic knowledge

Student needs to support actively Ichinen Bridport

Minimum training required for the orange belt is 4 months from yellow belt

A significant step for every student will be the green belt. Although commonly known as "half the black belt", the content is less than a quarter of what a black belt has to demonstrate.

3rd Kyu/Green belt

Break falls
roll forward, backward roll, roll sideways, all left and right
fall forward, -back and sideways and 2 rolls over an obstacle + 3 free choice

2 Foot throws + follow up technique

1 Hip throw + follow up technique

1 Shoulder throw + follow up technique

1 self falling technique

4 defences against strangle hold

4 strangling holds

3 hold downs + 2 liberations

3 transport grips

3 wrist locks

Throat nerve press, control attacker

3 arm locks

3 defences against bear hugs

3 Kicks

5 defences against various weapons/objects

3 uses of unnatural weapons

1 fight against minimum orange belt, 3 minutes

Defence against 2 attackers at same time, 2 minutes

Demonstrate one defence against the following situations:

1. One person pushes, hands to chest, followed by the pusher striking to the head.

2. A swinging punch to the head.

3. A front clothing grab, one handed, followed by a punch to the head / or a head butt

4. A front clothing grab, two hands, followed by the knee to the groin.

5. A bottle or glass to the head.

6. A lashing kick to the groin

7. A slash with knife

Theory:

-Judo = Japanese originated Budo system (Sport and personal education)

-Jiu-Jitsu = "the soft art", "winning by losing", an all-round martial art fighting system. Jiu-Jitsu is excellent for self defence.

-Karate = Japanese originated Budo system. Mainly hand and foot techniques, called "empty hand".

- Jiu-Jitsu grading system = white, yellow, orange, green, blue, brown, black.

-Natural + unnatural weapons -Self defence and the law

-12 Japanese terms

-Dojo etiquette

-First aid basic knowledge. Be familiar with the work sheets.

The minimum training required for the green belt is 4 months from the orange belt. Two martial art seminars or equal value grading in other systems are required since training began. The candidate must be able to run a class, including warm up.

You find additional information and updates on our Jiu-Jitsu blog online https://jiu-jitsuinbridport.blogspot.com/

A huge step is taken by achieving the 2nd Kyu blue belt. Not many students get this far and it is therefore very special to gain this status.

"You have to leave the comfort zone." (Wise words by Master Horst)

2nd Kyu/Blue belt

Break falls
roll forward, backward roll, roll sideways, all left and right
fall forward, -back and sideways and 3 rolls over an obstacle + 3 free
choice

3 break falls and rolls on hard floor

8 throws (variation of throws including follow up techniques)

5 defences against strangle hold

5 strangling holds

3 hold downs + 3 liberations

5 transport grips

4 wrist locks

Throat nerve press, control attacker

4 arm locks

4 defences against bear hugs

3 Kicks

5 defences against various weapons/objects

5 uses of unnatural weapons

1 fight against minimum orange belt, 3 minutes

Defence against 2 attackers at same time, 3 minutes

Demonstrate one defence against the following situations:

1. One person pushes, hands to chest, followed by the pusher striking to the head.

2. A swinging punch to the head.

3. A front clothing grab, one handed, followed by a punch to the head / or a head butt

4. A front clothing grab, two hands, followed by the knee to the groin.

5. A bottle or glass to the head.

6. A lashing kick to the groin

7. A slash with a knife

Theory:

1. What is Jiu-Jitsu?

2. Martial art / self defence and the law

   DBS (criminal record check in the UK), self defence

3. First aid / emergency

   In the dojo, on the streets, first aid basic knowledge

4. Anatomy

Bones, blood, nerves, vulnerable points

5.   Other martial arts

6.   Japanese terms

7.   Why are you practising Jiu-Jitsu?

     A personal view, good reasons

8.   How to run a Jiu-Jitsu session?

     Prepare hall, greet members, good time keeping, Health &
     Safety, warm up.

9.   Dojo etiquette

Japanese terminology for Jiu Jitsu / martial arts for the 2nd Kyu /
blue belt

1	Ichi
2	Ni
3	San
4	Shi
5	Go
6	Roku
7	Shichi
8	Hachi
9	Ku
10	Ju

Ashi   Leg or foot
Budo   Martial or military way or philosophy
Dan   Master Grade
Do   Way, philosophy, doctrine, reason, principle, virtue
        Dojo Commonly called a practice hall, but actually a place
        of meditation.

Gi   To dress, a garment (Always used as suffix as in Jiu-Jitsu Gi
Hajime Start (Used as a referee's command in contests)

Ju   The concept of "ju" is to be flexible, pliable, yielding or adaptive. It summarizes the philosophy of judo and jujutsu in which functional strength, flexibility and adaptability is emphasized, both physically and mentally. Jiu is equal, just different translation

Jutsu   Skill, art, technique

Ki   Vital force, internal energy, spirit

Kiai   A shout used to show spirit, often used when executing a technique. A good translation might be spirit shout or combat shout.

Mate   Wait, pause

O   Major, great, big

Rei   bow

Tatami Mat

Tori   Means to take. The person who performs the technique

Uke   To receive - The receiver in a technique

Yame   Stop

Minimum training required for the blue belt is 5 months from green belt. Three martial art seminars/contest or equal value grading in other system is required.

Student needs to support actively Ichinen Bridport

1st Kyu/Brown belt

"97% of the people who quit too soon are employed by the 3% who never gave up." (Wise words by Master Horst) Not very many have the stamina to get to this level.

Break falls
roll forward, backward roll, roll sideways, all left and right
fall forward, -back and sideways and 3 rolls over an obstacle + 3 free choice 3 break falls/ rolls on hard floor

12 throws (3 with follow up techniques)

7 strangling holds

6 defences against strangling

4 hold downs + 3 liberations

5 knife defences

2 gun defences

6 transport grips

6 wrist locks

Throat nerve press, control attacker

5 arm locks

5 defences against bear hugs

3 Kicks

Demonstration of Karate and boxing techniques

5 defences against various weapons/objects

5 uses of unnatural weapons

1 fight against minimum green belt, 3 minutes

Defences against 2 attackers at same time, 3 minutes

Collection of unnatural weapons for the grading

Demonstrate one defence against the following situations:

1. One person pushes, hands to chest, followed by the pusher striking to the head.

2. A swinging punch to the head.

3. A front clothing grab, one handed, followed by a punch to the head / or a head butt

4. A front clothing grab, two hands, followed by the knee to the groin.

5. A bottle or glass to the head.

6. A lashing kick to the groin

7. A slash with a knife

Theory:

1. What is Jiu-Jitsu?

   Different styles, history

2. Martial arts and the law

   DBS (criminal record check in UK), self defence

3. First aid / emergency

   In the dojo, in the streets

4. Anatomy

   Bones, blood, nerves, joints

5. Other martial arts, difference / comparison to Jiu-Jitsu

6. Japanese terms

   See special for brown belt

7. Why are you practising Jiu-Jitsu?

   A personal view, good reasons

8. How to run a Jiu-Jitsu session?

   Prepare hall, greet members, good time keeping, health & safety, warm up.

9. Dojo etiquette

10. Atemi points

Japanese terminology for Jiu Jitsu 1st Kyu / Brown belt

1	Ichi
2	Ni
3	San
4	Shi
5	Go
6	Roku
7	Shichi
8	Hachi
9	Ku
10	Ju

Ashi	Foot
Hiza	Knee
Shute	Palm of hand
Suigetsu	Solar Plexus
Tai	Body
Te	Hand
Tekubi	Wrist
Ude	Arm
Bo	Long wooden stick
Bokken	Wooden sword
Bu	Martial, military
Budo	Martial or military way or philosophy
Bujutsu	Martial skill or martial technique
Bushido	Way of the warrior. A code of conduct for the warrior class
Dan	Master grade

"Start with a dream." (Wise words by Master Horst)

Do	Way, philosophy, doctrine, reason, principle, virtue
Dojo	Commonly called a practice hall, but actually a place of meditation.
Empi	Elbow
Gi	To dress, a garment. As in Jiu-Jitsu Gi

Gyaku	Reverse
Hajime	To start, used as a referee's command in contests
Hakama	The loose trousers worn by the samurai. Today used in some martial arts.

Hara	The belly, often believed to be the center of the Ki.
Ichiban	Number one, the first/best
Judoka	One who practices judo
Ju	The concept of "ju" is to be flexible, pliable, yielding or adaptive. It summarizes the philosophy of judo and jiu-jitsu in which functional strength, flexibility and adaptability is emphasized, physically and mentally.

Jutsu, Jitsu	Skill, technique
Kata	A kata is a pre-arranged drill or exercise used for training purposes.
Ki	Vital force, internal energy, spirit
Kiai	A short yell used to show spirit, often used when executing a technique

Kumite	Sparring
Mate	Wait, pause
O	Major, great, big
O Sensei	Venerable teacher. The founder of aikido, Morihei Uyeshiba is the most famous person with the title of "O Sensei."

Obi	Belt
Randori	Free practice
Rei	To bow
Ritsurei	Standing bow

Tatami	Mat
Tori	Means to take. The person who performs the technique
Uke	To receive. The receiver in a technique
Uke	Blocking a punch or kick
Yame	Stop
Yoi	Command to get ready

Zarei	A seated, formal bow
Zen	Virtue, goodness
Zori	Sandals made of straw
Zubon	The trousers in a Jiu-Jitsu Gi

The candidate must be familiar with all the relevant worksheets from Ichinen Bridport.

Minimum training required for the brown belt is 7 months from the blue belt. Five martial art seminars/contest or equal value grading in other systems required.

Student needs to support actively Ichinen Bridport

Jiu-Jitsu /1st Dan syllabus

Introduction How long does it take to become a black belt? The answer is, a minimum of 36 months. After brown belt grading, there is usually a 10-month preparation period necessary.

In these 36 months you must have received training and tuition at least twice a week on average. In extraordinary circumstances, it is possible to shorten this time of preparation and readiness, for example, if the candidate has already proved that he/she is knowledgeable with the requirements and / or trains significantly more hours in a shorter period of time.

As the majority of students train for their black belt achievement more as a hobby, they collect about 1000 hours of training over three years of preparation. This is calculated on a regular twice-weekly training.

Another route to the black belt grading can be the more professional one. Here the student trains significantly more hours in a shorter period of time and reaches the same rate of improvement.

I personally took this path and trained for my black belt grading with more than 1,500 hours within a year. However I had had years of training before that already. Whichever path you choose, at the date of the grading, you need to know your stuff!

When I mentioned this preparation period of 36 months earlier on, it only gives you the average time people use in various martial art styles to gain black belt standard. Of course it is possible to reach that level earlier under the right supervision of a responsible Master and hard effort on your part.

Most importantly, you must devote yourself to your practice and work hard. A candidate for black belt will realize that training for the belt is not as important as the lessons learned along the way.

There is much more than just learning the physical skills and techniques. The learning includes conduct, character, discipline, mind power, endurance and internalization of the principles of Jiu-Jitsu. Application of these principles to life outside the dojo is one of the unifying commonalities that brings black belts of all styles together. As a black belt, you strive to apply all the principles you have learned in class to the rest of your life. For example, when you learn that you must be committed to a Jiu-Jitsu throw and follow through to make it work, as a black belt you should become conscious of how these same principles will help you to achieve other goals off the mat.

This is why the rank is earned by the student, but awarded by the sensei. Train hard, be humble, don't show off or complain! And always do the best in everything in your life. This is what it means to be a black belt. Black belts are often ordinary people who try harder and don't give up.

The black belt can be achieved in spite of any weaknesses you may have. I have promoted men and women who began training very late in life, people who were disabled and people who were very afraid of physical activity when they started. It is how you face and overcome your own personal difficulties that determines your character, an important component of a black belt.

The successful candidate has to master the following.

1. General attitude

2. Minimum age at Ichinen Bridport is 16 years

3. Proof of teaching students as an assistant

4. Students must have completed the club instructor course

5. Candidate must have first aid course.

6. Student needs to support actively Ichinen Bridport

7. Anatomical knowledge

8. Collection of own weapons used for grading

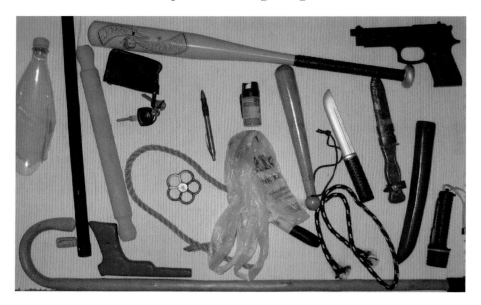

9. Seminars

10. 3 person attacks

11. Sparring - duration of at least 3 minutes

12. Demonstrate defence against 10 most common attacks

13. 1 Kata

14. Your own martial-art-related essay

15. Japanese terminology

16. Knowledge of Jiu-Jitsu history

17. No criminal records

18. Technical skills

Besides all of these requirements you have to be very fit to pass successfully a 1st Dan Jiu-Jitsu grading. Four months before I graduated in 1989, I ran the marathon distance (26.219 miles) in Bremen/Germany. The next photo shows me after my second marathon in Berlin/Germany. That was in the 1992. Bruce Lee used to say "running is best to keep fit".

Master Horst D. Lindenau after his 2nd Marathon in Berlin 1992

The black belt syllabus in detail

1. General attitude

The candidate must have the recommendation of their sensei. Before he/she is able to enter the black belt grading. Generally it applies what was pointed out in the introduction.

2. Minimum age

"As the black belt is not only a matter of certain technical or fitness skills, one can assume that a person over 16 years has got the character to give this rank a genuine meaning." This is a wide spread attitude in the martial arts world. But in Japan, where Jiu-Jitsu originated, children can achieve a black belt even at the age of six years. At Ichinen we are looking at the student and when he/she is ready the grade comes.

3. Proof of teaching students as an assistant.

This is certified by the Sensei of the school.

4. Students must have completed the club assistant instructor course.

This course is of very high importance. Too often we meet black belts, can be any Dan grade really, they have certain qualities which make them special. Some are good fighters and won a great number of competitions. Others are excellent technicians in the style of their art and can perform themselves on a very high quality level. Then we have those, they got the black belt and an excellent business talent and they run the martial arts school as it were any other business. What we unfortunately often miss are good teaching skills. Therefore at Ichinen Bridport the brown belt grade has to attend the school internal coaching course as a minimum study to learn about their later role as an instructor, when they run the own school.

This course is as follows:

- Attendance records

- 1. Aid and emergencies

- Warming up procedure

- Emergency phone no's

- Insurance

- Hall / dojo management

- Minimum grade

- DBS responsibilities, vulnerable students

- Valuables

- Training procedures / exclusions

- Weapons

- Visitors

- Activity record

- New students

- Risk assessment / safe environment

- General teaching skills

- Children and vulnerable people / special needs

- Anatomy

- Head organisation

- School assistance

This is certified by the Sensei of the school.

Deliver certificate/record book.

5. Candidate must have first aid certificate.

Deliver certificate/record book.

6. School engagement

Candidate is knowledgeable and engaged in the daily routine of running the martial art school.

"A black belt should be loyal to his Sensei." (Wise words by Master Horst)

7. Anatomical Knowledge

Good knowledge of the human body regarding the martial arts and self defence.

8. Collection of own weapons (natural and unnatural):

E.g. pistol, bottle, short stick, long stick, rope, knife, baseball bat, carrier bag, key ring, belt, walking stick.

9. Seminars

Minimum of 6 martial arts seminars

10.   3-person attacks

    Armed and unarmed, 3 minutes

11.   Sparring - duration of at least 3 minutes

12.   Demonstrate defence against 10 most common attacks

1.   One person pushes, hands to chest, which is normally followed by the pusher striking first, to the head.

2.   A swinging punch to the head.

3.   A front clothing grab, one handed, followed by a punch to the head.

4.   A front clothing grab, two hands, followed by a head butt.

5.   A front clothing grab, two hands, followed by a knee to the groin.

6.   A bottle, glass, or ashtray to the head.

7.   A lashing kick to the groin or lower legs.

8.   A broken bottle or glass jabbed to face.

9.   A slash with knife, most commonly a 3" to 4" lock-blade knife or kitchen utility knife.

10. A grappling-style head lock.

13. Kata

1 or 2 Kata, depending on difficulty

14. Original martial arts-related essay. Minimum of 500 words.

15. Japanese terminology

This is a brief list of the terminology for Jiu-Jitsu

Ashi	Foot
Hiza	Knee
Shute	Palm of hand
Suigetsu	Solar Plexus
Tai	Body
Te	Hand
Tekubi	Wrist
Ude	Arm
1	Ichi
2	Ni
3	San
4	Shi
5	Go
6	Roku
7	Nana

8	Hachi
9	Ku
10	Ju

Atemi	To strike a person
Bo	Long wooden stick
Bokken	Wooden sword
Bu	Martial, military
Budo	Martial or military way or philosophy
Bujutsu	Martial skill or martial technique
Bushido	"Way of the warrior" A code of conduct for the warrior class

Dan	Grade
Do	Way, philosophy, reason, principle, virtue Road, way, or the right way or course of conduct
Dojo	Commonly called a practice hall
Eri	Lapel or collar of a Gi

Empi	Elbow
Gi	To dress, a garment. Used as suffix as in Jiu-Jitsu Gi
Gyaku	Reverse
Hajime	To start
Hakama	The loose trousers worn by the samurai and now used in some martial arts.

Hara	The belly, centre of Ki energy
Ichiban	Number one, the best
Judoka	One who practices judo, a student of judo
Ju	The concept of "ju" is to be flexible, pliable, yielding or adaptive. It summarizes the philosophy of judo and Jiu-Jitsu in which functional strength, flexibility and adaptability is emphasized, both physically and mentally.

Kata	Form. A kata is a pre-arranged drill or exercise used for training purposes.

Goshin Jitsu Form of self-defence art

Ki   Vital force, internal energy, spirit

Kiai   A short yell used to show spirit, often used when
            executing a technique.
Kumite   Sparring

Mate   Wait, pause
Mokuso   Mokuso is a Japanese term for Meditation, especially
            when practiced in the traditional Japanese martial arts.
        Mokuso (pronounced as "mohk so" or sometimes
        "mokuso") is performed before and after the Jiu-Jitsu
        session. With Mokuso we begin our training and
        concentrate on what's coming and leave the outer
        world out of our mind and out of the dojo. After the
        session we kind of seal what we have done and
        meditate on our progress and prepare for daily life
        continuing.

O   Major, great, big

O Sensei   Venerable teacher
Obi   Belt
Randori   Free practice
Rei   To bow
Ritsurei   Standing bow
Tai   Body

Tatami   Mat
Te   Hand
Tori   Means to take. The person who performs the technique
Uke   To receive - The receiver in a technique
Uke   Blocking a punch or kick
Yame   Stop

Yoi   Command to get ready
Zarei   A seated, formal bow
Zanshin   Alertness
Zen   Virtue, goodness

| Zori | Sandals made of straw |
| Zubon | The pants of a Jiu-Jitsu GI |

16. Knowledge of Jiu-Jitsu history

Original essay, minimum of 500 words

17. No criminal records / DBS check (in UK)

18. Technical skills

1. Complete rolls and break falls:

Forwards, backwards, left and right sides

Single side: 8 free choice, + rolls on hard floor

2. 14 throws

3. 8 wrist locks

4. 4 releases from wrist grabs

5. 6 releases from body grabs

6. 7 releases/defences from strangling

7. 5 release from bear hugs

8. 3 releases from head locks

9. 6 arm locks

10. 2 releases from arm locks

11. 5 transport holds

12. 2 releases from transport holds

13. 8 knife defences

14. 6 stick defences

15. 6 holds on the ground

16. 3 releases from holds on the ground

17. 4 defences against a punch

18. 5 strangle holds

19. 5 defences against kicking

20. 4 kicks

21. 4 gun defences

22. 2 shoulder locks

23. 6 feet / leg locks

24. 3 each: hand, fist, elbow strikes

25. 4 defences on ground

26. 7 manipulations at vulnerable points

27. 4 finger locks

28. 4 combinations

This is the grading syllabus in use at Ichinen Bridport in 2019. In comparison to other Jiu-Jitsu/Ju Jitsu organizations this ranks very highly. Many of the others are either too Judo oriented or are missing our focus on self defence. However, each version has got its own merits and there are different ways to approach a mastership.

Our training syllabus holds a lot of techniques that contribute to randori and competitions. Primarily those skills are useful in a self-defence situation and contribute to an all round education for the Jiu-Jitsuka. Although we do a lot of randori within the club, we have not had the chance to take part in any competitions yet. The reason is very simple: there are no similar Jiu-Jitsu clubs nearby and students avoid long journeys.

I have been thinking for some time now of replacing this system of general tasks to be worked on with one individual task. The student would perform for a certain length of time (for example blue belt 35 minutes) and demonstrate all his knowledge. This would be a free choice, according to student's sex, age, personal handicaps and preferences.

In my opinion there is absolutely no reason why a grading has to be performed in any particular way just to please an industry. There have always been various ranks among warriors and today's belt and colour system has only been in use for some 100 years. Modern systems such as the self defence BlackCombat use only a white and brown belt for the student grades, followed by a black belt for master grades. This is very much the same as it used to be in ancient Japan.

Of course this is only a thought at the moment. Another consideration is that any rank achieved needs to be comparable with that of other styles, otherwise the system would be diluted too much. This is not my intention nor am I entitled to do so. However, nothing is static and time will tell.

Time is also relevant for training and development. I trained from 4th kyu to black belt within 12 months, where I dedicated 24/7 of my time and recources into it. Then I stayed a 1st Dan black belt for 27 years before I reached the 2nd Dan. Now, at the age of 65, I still perform exeptonally well and whatever I teach, I can do myself. Honestly, I want to keep it like this, as I believe I have to be the living example for my students. So they can trust me. This is my way with Jiu-Jitsu.

"If you ever lack the motivation to train, then watch what happens to your body and mind when you don't." (Wise words by Master Horst)

The syllabus for minors is different from the above and is not listed in this book. At my school, certain students, who join at a more mature age, might be allowed to replace some of the required techniques like fighting/randori with Kata and similar skills. Jiu-Jitsu is for everyone, any age and the tasks can be adjusted to suit people's needs. This does not mean, they have it any easier or "watered down". They still do their full duty. This is the grading syllabus of my school Ichinen Bridport/UK in the year 2019.

Frequently asked questions

If you have never been in a martial arts club and if you are thinking of joining a Jiu-Jitsu club for the first time, here are some answers to FAQ.

Q: What is Jiu-Jitsu?

Jiu-Jitsu is a Japanese originated martial art which combines blocking, striking, throwing, choking, kicking, joint locking and ground techniques.

Jiu-Jitsu can be called "the mother of martial arts" (Japanese origin). The known styles of Judo, Aikido and Karate were formed from ancient Jiu-Jitsu. Jiu-Jitsu today is a mixture of all these other martial arts and more.

Jiu-Jitsu may be spelt in various following ways: ju jitsu, ju jutsu, jiu jitsu or jiu jutsu. Whichever way it is spelt, it means the same. The term "Jiu-Jitsu" literally means art (jitsu/jutsu) of flexibility. All these terms represent a single principle - the general way of applying a technique, of using the human body as a weapon in any combat. It too can be called "the soft art" or "winning by losing".

Q: Can I have a look at the session before joining?

Yes of course you can. At Ichinen Bridport we have an open door policy and anybody is welcome to watch our classes. Most schools do the same.

Q: When can I start as a total beginner?

You can start at any time. The lessons will be structured to your needs and capabilities. In Jiu-Jitsu there are usually no beginner courses as anybody can join in at any stage.

Q: What do I wear to start with?

Wear something loose and comfortable. A T-shirt and tracksuit bottoms, or any Gi from other martial arts practice will do. At Ichinen Bridport we wear plain black socks on the mat for hygiene. If you have a grade in a different martial art already, you have to wear a white belt to begin with. This indicates you are a beginner in Jiu-Jitsu, this will protect you being asked to do more than you are able to do.

Q: How much does it cost to train Jiu-Jitsu?

The first two lessons at Ichinen Bridport (2019) are £ 10 each. This is for 1.5 hours training each session. Often people point out, that others offer free taster sessions. Well, why should it be that way? Ever heard of first taxi ride free or first shopping free?

Q: Do I need to be fit before I start?

You can join at any level, as long as there are no real medical issues that stops you. Fitness should be no barrier to start Jiu-Jitsu. You will become fit by training in our style.

During training and little by little over time you will develop in various fields. The fitness level will rise and your stamina increases. You build up strength as well as speed in your movements and by executing the new techniques you learn. Most important besides the physical effects like better suppleness you will build up a great deal of mental improvement.

Q: What about age, does it matter?

No, it does not matter at all. We run classes for children (6-14) and adults (14-67 at present) and there is no age limit. And Jiu-Jitsu does not rely on physical strength. People of all ages, shapes and sizes can begin the training, men the same as women. You will always get involved in the kind of skills that suit your abilities. Not only age related. Sure, a teenager trains differently from a more mature person at the age of 55. Both learn the skills which suits them.

Q: Is Jiu-Jitsu suitable for women?

Yes of course it is. There is no difference versus men. The training syllabus might differ in small areas but generally it will be most similar.

Q: Can I do grading?

Yes you can. Ranks with coloured belts are used as an indicator of progress, knowledge and experience. Refer to our syllabus for more information. I would not recommend any martial arts training which does not involve a grading system. The grading system gives you a clear idea where you stand and what your next goal will be.

Q: Are my previous experiences in other martial arts recognized? We welcome martial artists from any discipline. As Jiu-Jitsu is a very flexible and all round style system, every skill will add to the whole. You will adapt Jiu-Jitsu specific way as you continue.

How to organize your training

At our school you can take part twice a week in any style we teach. The student can decide which session he likes to attend regularly and should then stick to it. It is very important to keep a routine; either attend on the first day or the second. Or choose both. Never leave it open to a choice. The human mind is easily distracted and you might say, "Oh, I'll go next time". When I was training to become a gym instructor, we were told that to run a professional gym the ideal opening hours would be 24/7. That makes it possible to sign up more students/customers than places available. However, everybody sits at home and says, "I'll go tomorrow…"

When you find your routine, stick to it!

Discipline is hard work, but worth keeping

Stone of courage in the former Japanese Zen garden which was built in Symondsbury by Master Horst and his students in 1994

When you begin training, you might like to keep your own records of it, a kind of a training diary. This way not only gives you a good idea of what you have done, but also what is still coming in the future to be learned. You can note down things like what you've learned, how you exercised, who your training partner was and so on, including your fitness level. Adding this to your practical training will give you a good understanding of your own efforts and can motivate you a lot.

For those that cannot attend at the regular evening classes or people that prefer individual training, I offer at Ichinen Bridport a wide range of private lessons. This is for both, adults and children as well.

The advantages of private lessons

Many students prefer that they can train at times that suits them better. This can be daytime and weekends if required. The student has got the chance to train significantly more hours rather than attending just the regular weekly session. This leads of course to better and faster progress in certain fields. By doing so, the minimum training times can be shortened if the quality of the skills is adequate. And any private student can attend the regular classes additional for free.

Often I see with students that they treat their involvement in the martial arts more professionally and less as another hobby. This focus can be supported with private tuition. And often the private student is stronger focused on personal goals for example to gain a certain grade or some special knowledge.

I had students that just wanted to add some grappling to their skills to become better in MMA fights. Others have a goal and need some education in self defence, as they plan to join the forces or work in the security industry.

And 1 to 1 personal training can change your life. To become the person you've always wanted to be and become the best version of yourself.

And it's not all about Jiu-Jitsu or martial arts. I have students that concentrate on meditation, some practice Yoga and others just need assistance with weight loss. Improved fitness and better looking / body shape can be another reason. You can find out if private tuition would improve your progress here
https://ichinenbridport.com/2019/01/17/the-benefits-of-11-training/

"People either find a way – or they find an excuse." (Wise words by Master Horst)

Competitions in Jiu-Jitsu

Did you take part in competitions? Countless times students and even outsiders have asked me that question. Yes I did compete. I have done Karate club fights in Bremen/Germany, Judo fights in Southampton/UK and once I took part at the North German Championships in Jiu-Jitsu. After this event, all that my Grandmaster had to say to me was: "Are you crazy? There is a risk you might get injured and are off training for three months! As a school teacher this is not a good thing to do." His second objection was the fact that, if you fight as a school teacher and lose, next you will lose many students. They just don't want to be with the loser. He didn't have to worry: in my case I was lucky and became North German champion. But it was hard to do as I was already 39 years old and the five fights I had to take on were against younger guys in their twenties.

Ok, after all I am not a great fan of competitions. As many other sports events are rigged today, you find the same sadly in the martial arts world. I witnessed one case myself, when the mother, who was a judge in the committee, put her son in a different order for his fight. So he could stand a chance. And, if I think of European championships, where only three nations take part and some participants just have to fight once to come out as European champion, I cannot agree with such a system. Instead of there being one world champion in a martial art, there seem to be 99 world champions each winning their own "world championship" competition.

But then I might surprise you. Now at an advanced age and no worries anymore if I would lose students at my school and even could cope with a "three months break" due to injury – I might join some competitions. Just to prove the point that Jiu-Jitsu can be like good wine. As older as better! I will let you know.

At Ichinen Bridport we are practising randori and competition fighting too. But so far, no one ever wanted to join any tournament.

It is quite an effort to travel half the country and stay somewhere over night. Many avoid that cost.

To practise randori or enter combat sports competitions there are special rules to consider. Important to know are the various banned actions for randori and fights in Jiu-Jitsu.

The Jiu-Jitsu style as we practise it includes randori and combat sport which requires a high degree of fairness and technical perfection. Since the Jiu-Jitsu fight on the mat only takes place in the region of the dedicated marked area, the forced activity of the fighters requires the utmost concentration and reaction. Therefore, banned actions must be stopped immediately by the referee.

These banned actions are basically introduced to keep the sometimes very vigorous fight safe and fair. Unfair techniques can be such as:

- Jerky or bumping movements at the partner.

- Cover the face with the body. The face must remain free.

- Attack or grab ears, nose, hair, fingers or toes.

- Kicks, punches, push with force, hit and press in the face or face tears is forbidden.

- Talking when on the mat.

- Dirty gestures or remarks against the opponent or referee.

- Pull the back of the spine over the spine.

- Press or throw the opponent over the white line outside the marked area.

- Avoid the fight or escape behind the white line.

All techniques outside the white line are marked with a warning.

Prohibited actions are immediately punished by the referee with a warning and the opponent immediately receives a point.

My idea of competing is the street fighting experience. And here, I must confess I have a good record. From my perspective, this is the real proof that your style works for self defence and you can make use of it when needed. This applies of course only for those styles that focus on self defence. There is a huge difference in applying a technique in a sports contest or real life situations.

Master Horst D. Lindenau on the right

Some practical ideas for randori and competition fighting

Always keep full attention focused on the opponent. Look at his upper body, head, shoulders, that's where you identify his moves quickest. Keep good observation and monitoring all the time. Never underestimate your opponent. It is quite common that a 4th Kyu takes a black belt to the mat because the Dan grade assumed their higher ranking meant they were better. Be aware that half of the game is in your mind. Therefore control your mind.

Which tactic you use in a fight is a rather personal choice. I prefer the "Blitz". Which means I pretend being more defensive and hit out of the blue. I once asked Don Wilson (10 times Kick boxing world champion) what his strategy was and he said, he tires them out: "Six to eight rounds of quick and fast engagement and then a knock out next round. You need to be fit for that!"

The more counter skills fighting you can master, the better. As there is a counter to every attack. Last but not least: do not enter a competition without very good preparation. I know of some teachers that send their students right into the fire. You lose and don't learn anything other than to lose.

Jiu-Jitsu for children

Teaching children is essential if a master takes his dedication to the martial arts seriously. There are two reasons for this. The first reason is that children are like the ambassadors for Jiu-Jitsu. What they learn at a young age will stay with them all their lives and each child benefits from it a great deal.

A child benefits from physical (and spiritual) education and today's technological world means children seem to be getting less and less active and more and more focused on a computer interface. Jiu-Jitsu can provide physical and mental stimulation and helps to develop the positive energy in a child.

The second reason is simple, that if you start teaching, the real learning and understanding comes through it. And teaching children is an extra challenge as it requires more than just a few martial arts skills. You need to be a solid person yourself. Stable enough to give the young ones a good example and act like a light house for them. They will always remember you!

Children learn much faster and easier than students who have passed their youth. It comes easy to them, as with any other knowledge, they act like a sponge when presented with new skills.

Teaching children has a lot more responsibility. Not only do you need good knowledge of first aid for the young ones, you also need a DBS check (in the UK for child protection by law) and you have to be extra careful, as children are still growing mentally and physically and therefore the whole range of Jiu-Jitsu isn't appropriate for them.

It is a wonderful feeling, when you walk down the street and a man in his 30s stops you and says hello. And you don't recognize him, as he has changed a lot since he was your student 20 years ago. And even better is, if that man brings his own boy later to your children's class.

Technically there is a separate syllabus for children. For many years I was strictly against this new modern way of graduating young children as a black belt at the age of nine. I thought this was just the disease of commerce arriving in the martial arts. But as they say, the older you get – the wiser you become… and I have changed my opinion over this controversy.

Children too can have private 1:1 lessons at Ichinen Bridport Jiu-Jitsu

Children's Dan - black belt for children

Recently we have changed the attitude towards the grading of black belts for minors at Ichinen Bridport. They can graduate at any time once they are competent in techniques for the relevant grade. Once the pass the age of 16 years, then an additional grading transfers their knowledge and progress into the common black belt standard of the adult level.

For a long time in Germany, the idea of a black belt for children was impossible. People would claim it was not the tradition and also claim that a black belt must come with certain kind of mental maturity.

But - and this important point is overlooked by all critics. The invention of the children's Dan is by no means a western invention. In the great martial arts mother countries, whether of Korean, Chinese or Japanese origin, black belts for children are not uncommon.

Consequently we have changed our requirements here at Ichinen Bridport and children can gain their black belt, as long they fulfill what is required by the syllabus. One reason for this is in the country of origin of Jiu-Jitsu, they have always done so.

Another reason for allowing a children's Dan grade is what I consider to be what the belt represents, balanced with what has to be done to attain it. And here I believe that in the past the status has been exaggerated and given too much importance.

Often, to justify rigorous examination requirements, to substantiate allegedly necessary intermediate examinations, or even to let unwelcome persons fail on the grounds of an inappropriate, inadequate or weak mental attitude during the examination, the myth was invented for the requirement of mental maturity for the acquisition of the black belt, which naturally prevented children from achieving it.

The first black belt is only the first step on a long journey with no end. It marks the last of the coloured belts and opens the path to even more studies. From now on, the belt colour does not change until one reaches the 6th Dan grade. In this regard, there is no reason to reject black belts for children from the outset.

How do you explain to children logically that they cannot make a Dan, when they see clearly that their techniques are better than those of the lanky 22-year-old or the somewhat obese 35-year-old?

Why is the 55-year-old allowed to make a Dan grade, even though he might not perform different techniques properly, or the 70-year-old, who can put far less power into his techniques than the 16 year old teenager?

It's time to put an end to old unfounded judgements. We should not turn the black belt into something more special than it is. Anyone who meets the technical and mental requirements should also be able to reach the black belt without artificial restrictions. At the end of the day there is a big difference between a master and a Sensei. And that has little to do with the colour of the belt.

My own way

The most common of many questions people ask me about my career in Jiu-Jitsu is, when did you first start? This is a little bit of a social and psychological matter. If you say I have done it since I was a young child, people assume you are out dated by now. If you say I have been doing it for the last seven years they look at you as a really determined guy who took a quick way up to success. I personally find this question nonsense. A little bit like comparing an old banger with a brand new BMW.

Anyway, here is my answer. My first step into the martial arts world was at the age of nine years old. I joined the local Judo club which held sessions once a week in the recreation hall of my preschool. I loved it! The judo mats had to be laid out to begin with and they were that heavy that it took four of us to carry them down the stairs.

They were hard as concrete!

I did six months of very enthusiastic and enjoyable training but when it came to the first grading, I had to stop. My family couldn't afford to buy the Gi which was compulsory for the grading and that stopped me going. Today it is hard to understand, as the cost of the equipment now is next to nothing. And because of my own experience with this children can train with us any time without Gi and even do the first two grading in casual wear.

Ten years later I had the chance to look inside a modern Japanese dojo in Yokohama. I was so impressed with the atmosphere, the discipline and the people I met that it put a seed in my head.

From then on my interest increased and during my first years at sea I tried to visit a martial arts school wherever we went. Hong Kong, Kaohsiung in Taiwan, Singapore and Manila in the Philippines were stations where I tried to pick up some skills and ideas. We used to have our own punch bag in the pump room on board one ship and I remember the training and long runs we did when in port with my later martial arts friend master Mark Horemans from Sussex/England who is a Wado Ryu Karateka.

The real learning, though, came with the real fights. These were hard lessons. Every harbour has got a red light district, and believe me, we did not miss one out. So, my first gun defence was done in Pusan, Korea. At the time I did not realize that I did just the right thing. Looked into the barrel of the gun and paid the money they asked for. It saved my life!

I was not so successful on Tenerife. Three black guys decided to change the owner of my watch and wallet and, after a fierce fist fight, they got it and ran off, leaving me covered in blood and a few Pesetas poorer.

I guess my master piece in those days happened at Kingston in Jamaica. We had been told not to go to the Casa Verde club, which I did straight away. And oh, I tell you, at the door was this beauty taking the entrance fee and I asked her if she could come in with me, which she did, after passing the till job to her friend. Inside was the most steaming ambience and intensive atmosphere you can imagine.

It was nearly pitch black too. When I noticed that I was surrounded by six local men sitting at our table, I thought this is the end. I must admit, I was the only white guy in this club and the natives there are on average 6" 12", which is seven feet. I was scared!

I knew that to get out of there alive, or at least in one piece, it needed a drastic move. I asked one of them to get the biggest knife from the kitchen, which he did. Then I placed the knife on my forearm and told them that we are all brothers as we all have the same red blood I said I will be the one to cut me open first and I looked around to find the first one of them to do the same. But then the leader of the gang stopped me just putting the blade to my skin and gave me a manly hug and passed me his whisky and a big smoke. Life is a fight!

The favelas in Rio de Janeiro, where I spent a fortnight, were more like a game. We just dressed like the locals and being able to speak some Portuguese helped a lot as we were taken as some locals. Down there it is a bit like New Years Eve in Germany. Bang – bang – bang! And no, it wasn't the New Year's Eve fire crackers. This bang – bang – bang goes on each night and even daytime. They were just shooting at each other all over the place. From our crew on board of 65 men, fourteen got robbed and mugged in fourteen days! Not me. Self defence begins with assessing the situation, avoid the dark spots and be more like a Ninja. Dress like the crowd, move like the crowd and be smart.

Well, another place to learn a bit of street and pub fighting was Barranquilla in Colombia. By the way that was the place of my first real wedding engagement. In that town people are so poor, someone would have killed you for any possession. But I survived three visits to this wonderful place. Mind you, I had sort of family protection.

Manila, the capital of the Philippines was a town you could not walk around freely without armed friends in those days. Every, and I mean every, bar, shop or smallest establishment had an armed guard inside and outside. Only on our boat, we got 50 armed guards during the stay. You have to learn how to move right if you want to survive but have some fun too.

In those days fighting and violence were present in daily life. Today's club doormen have to be trained and qualified and are not allowed anymore to touch a customer who stirs up some trouble. All is on CCTV and everybody will have a lawyer to sue after an alleged assault. In the old days, when I did my journeys all over the globe, a bouncer, as the doormen were called, could easily beat the pulp out of someone starting trouble. Also police could be corrupt and might be the ones who robbed you.

I'll never forget our young 3rd officer returning from ashore and he was crying. Two policemen had asked him to join their car and they drove him to the outskirts of Manila, just to empty his pockets. By the way, on the same voyage our captain returned back to the boat, him and his wife stripped completely naked. Their lives had only just been saved and their dignity saved by paper cement bags they found in the street. The degree and quality of someone's self defence skills have always to meet the actual situation and time.

I was overall rather lucky that I never had any big losses or got physically hurt. A little fight here and there is not worth mentioning.

I started to visit martial arts sessions where ever it was possible. One must understand that in the 70s there was much less Budo and martial arts around in most places. Some people had boxing clubs and often combined them with some kind of Jujutsu and Karate. Similarly Kung Fu was on the rise. Today I believe there is more Japanese style martial arts outside Japan than in the country of origin itself.

Whenever I stayed ashore for a while to do further education at high school, work in the docks or in a dock yard, I took the chance and joined martial arts clubs for regular training in my home town Bremen in Germany.

I was now focused on Karate, as that was the style I learned my first lessons after Judo. It was four years later at the age of 14 and the guy who trained us was called "Pfeil", which means "arrow" in German. He was a 1st Kyu brown belt at that time. Actually his brother "Wau Wau" was there too and such is life, I met him only last year again. My niece in Bremen/Germany is now one of his students and she has a 2nd Kyu blue belt Shotokan Karate already.

Later, I joined a school in Bremen, Langenstrasse and trained Shotokan Karate and Judo for 12 months. This stopped, however, when I became a sailor and left my home town.

In 1977 I joined the Budo-Club Bremen. This was the best thing I believe that could have happened to me. The teacher then was Wolf-Dieter Wichmann, a 3rd Dan Shotokan Karate, who later became world champion by beating the Japanese team. Looking back, I was very lucky to have had him as a teacher. He laid the foundation for my enthusiasm in Budo which is still in me. I left the Budo-Club after two years as a green belt 6th Kyu Shotokan and went back to the ships.

In 1987 a friend took me to his club ATKSB in Bremen (Anti-Terrorkampf school Blumenthal). The style they trained there impressed me instantly, as my Karate Gi was ripped apart after the first session! This style was called Anti-Terrorkampf (Anti Terror Combat) and beside that they offered Jiu-Jitsu, which I attended too.

This training was very different from what I had done before. I would say there was much less Budo but more hard core self defence.

Through this membership, I met Grand master Horst Weiland †, who was the President of their martial arts organization called BAE and I knew instantly that I was going to learn with him. Not long after, my family, with our two boys, moved up north and I joined the BAE (Budo-Akademie-Europa) for private training to become a professional diploma sports teacher for martial arts under supervision of Grand master Horst Weiland †.

I had to sign on for one year (365 days!) with daily training and it was agreed, if I failed to attend a single day, the game was over. This was a most intensive program. Training was five days a week for eight hours a day and 40 out of 52 weekends of that year I had to attend seminars all over Germany.

In this year I studied Anti-Terrorkampf, Jiu-Jitsu, Judo, Shotokan Karate, All style Do Karate, Ajukate, Taekwondo, Kung Fu, Fight of knife, Mebethe and Yoga and fitness/gym training.

Training included education in how to run your own school with a focus of teaching children. Today I still benefit from this great knowledge of my Grand master Horst Weiland † and his team at the BAE headquarters. It was the very best one could get. Big honour and respect!

After that year, I graduated as a diploma sports teacher for Jiu-Jitsu, Karate, Anti-Terrorkampf (Anti Terror Combat), Ajukate (All style martial art), Close-Combat (Survival training) and Yoga. My written thesis was about modern technology in the promotion of martial arts and how to use video techniques for that.

I graduated finally in two styles and became a 1st Dan Jiu-Jitsu and a 1st Dan Anti-Terrorkampf. I was 35 years old that time.

"Make time to practice meditation and Yoga." (Wise words by Master Horst)

The author with his late Grand master Horst Weiland † Germany
10th Dan Jiu-Jitsu

In 1989 I moved back to my home town Bremen to open the first own martial arts school. The SDS Bremen (Studio of Self Defence Bremen).

The start wasn't easy in those days. I will never forget when I gave the first session with only two students and the big disappointment after these two didn't turn up for the second session. There was no support whatsoever from my old club which was nearby, as the teacher there was just too jealous and couldn't bear me running my own school now.

This experience should be useful in the future on many occasions. Competitors in business can be jealous sometimes, but in the martial arts world this is far more widespread. It has to do with the fact, that someone who picks up a martial arts discipline and makes their way up to a master degree often has a weak ego or spiritual mind to begin with. As there is none or little education in most organisations where it is fore mostly a sport, the mind, the spiritual side of the arts are neglected.

By the way, one former teacher of Jiu-Jitsu didn't even congratulate me for the grading and he even tried to make me fail at a later grading years later, where he sat on the panel. Well, not every teacher you pass in life is a bonanza. You have to be selective yourself, as soon you can see where your own journey leads you to.

You soon will learn, not each "black belt" is a master. Learn your own lessons and try to be good. If you are better today than yesterday then you are going the right direction. Life takes small steps but forward if you do your tasks.

You overcome all these obstacles and I went on with my own way, as I was taught by my Grand master and many other true masters I would study with in later years. I will not name anyone here, but I can assure you that I was lucky and had the chance to train with masters all over the globe, highly decorated martial arts experts and even world champions.

My Studio for Self Defence in Bremen (SDS Bremen) boomed within the next three months and I could register the 50th student. I was offering Jiu-Jitsu for adults and children, Anti-Terrorkampf and Yoga only for adults. It was always important to keep the connection between the hard styles and the soft in balance. Later in 1996 I graduated as a Yoga teacher with the Birinsi-Institute in Utrecht / Netherlands. I personally know only five people in my life who mastered a martial arts black belt and became a Yoga master too. One of them was my German Grand master Horst Weiland †.

My personal way with combining the two worlds of martial arts and Yoga has done a great deal for me. I could establish a fine path, which still gives me safe guidance through this sometimes hectic and demanding life we live nowadays.

Regarding hard and softer style I like to tell you a little anecdote. One night after the Jiu-Jitsu session a man entered the dojo and asked if he could rent some space and time for his own training of Muay Thai. We agreed as this helped me to cover the costs to run the place.

Later at home I couldn't stop thinking, that I knew this man from the past. And I did, it turned out that he was Klaus Handke, who I shared training of Shotokan Karate some 20 years before. I thought this meeting again was meant to be by destiny.

Later at some point I joined one of his classes and to be honest, this was the first and only time I stopped training. Not because of his teaching, he was absolutely great and superb in what he did, but it was just too tough for me. I thought "they kill each other". Real Muay Thai fighting is the toughest you can hit in martial arts. And Klaus was the very first westerner who became a Thai box champion in Thailand ever.

At the age of 39 I made a silly decision and took part in the North

German Jiu-Jitsu competitions. Grand master Weiland asked me afterwards, if I became crazy now to take part in that contest. What he meant was, in case I would have lost, my students would have left me as no one wants to learn from a loser. Or I could have been injured, which would have put my school at risk as I was the head coach. In those days only my wife was assisting me as a brown belt.

The Grand master was right, but today as I type these words and I am 64 years of age now, I think of entering another competition again. Why not? Age is just a number when you stay fit with your Jiu-Jitsu skills. And these times I even don't care if I had to close down my school for a certain time … just in case.

Three years passed quickly and I could congratulate my first student who passed his black belt grading. My Grand master Horst Weiland † who watched the graduations in those days as a "visitor" said to me later: "In the student, you recognize the master". I couldn't get a better compliment towards my teaching and today I am still proud of it and this influences my daily routine with the school and teaching in general.

This new black belt took over my SDS Bremen and I left the country to settle down in the UK. His name is Frank Burdorf and he is teaching the art of Jiu-Jitsu in Bremen and is today a 6th Dan.

Since then a lot has happened. I have been teaching all over the place. After four years in the UK I went back to Germany. This time to Berlin for two years to teach Jiu-Jitsu and Ant-Terrorkampf. Besides that we were developing "Glima", a pagan style martial art with my Berlin friend and homeopathic doctor Uwe Ecker. He was the chairman of the Berlin pagans and with him and another friend we founded "Glima Germany" on the 24.07.1997.

Unfortunately Uwe's fiancée had a bad accident and burnt heavily, which stopped the further development of the Glima project. After that I returned back to my home town Bremen and taught for two years in a local sport centre the art of Jiu-Jitsu and another group at the Bremen Jacobs University.

Today my home is in England and here I run the oldest club in a small country town in the South West of the country called Bridport. This is the Ichinen Bridport martial arts school.

I would always rate the Jiu-Jitsu style and system as probably the best basis for any martial artist. Why? Simply because it combines the ground work with standing moves, punches, kicks, locks and throws, but also a spiritual side with honour and respect. And the one, who doesn't inherit this side, will always fail.

What is Ichinen?

Determination, decisiveness and purposefulness, Ichinen

Years ago I have chosen the word Ichinen for my activities. My martial arts school, which was first called "Studio for self defence" became now Ichinen. To give it a specific title I added the location and therefore it is called Ichinen Bridport.

First own Dojo in the Southwest of England. **Ichinen Bridport**

Ichinen is a Japanese word, meaning determination. As it is in the Japanese language this translation is amongst other things. This one explains best what it stands for.

Being good at something is not just about talent. It is about having the desire, in your heart to make it happen. If you have a strong Ichinen, you will reach your goal. You still have to put in the effort and in fact, the more talent you have, the more effort is needed, because your end result might be far more ambitious than for a less talented person.

"Learn self control – than you master yourself easy." (Wise words by Master Horst)

You give every effort. And only you decide when you have failed. A German proverb says: "Nur wer aufgibt hat verloren!" This sums it all up. Only the one who gives up has lost.

In the Wikipedia directory we find this information:

Ichinen: (一念) (Japanese: Chin *i-nien*)

> Ichinen is a single moment of life, one instant of thought, or the mind or life at a single moment. It is also, life-moment, thought-moment, or simply a single moment or instant.

> Ichinen has various meanings in Buddhism:

> 1. It can be a moment, or an extremely short period comparable to the Sanskrit term Kshana. The treatise on the great perfection of wisdom defines one Kshana or moment as a sixtieth of the time it takes to snap one's fingers. Wow!

> 2. The functioning of the mind for one moment. The "Distinctions in Benefits" 17th chapter of the Lotus Sutra speaks of a single moment of belief and understanding.

> 3. To focus one's mind on meditating on a Buddha; Shan-Tao (613-681), a patriarch of the Chinese Pure Land school, defined Ichinen (one instant of thought) as chanting Amida Buddha's name once.

> 4. T'ient'ai (538-597) philosophically interprets Ichinen in his doctrine of three thousand realms in a single moment of life (Japanese Ichinen-Sanzen Chin i-nien san-ch'ien). In this doctrine, Ichinen indicates the mind of an ordinary person, which at each moment is endowed with the potential of three thousand realms; its characteristics are:

> A: it pervades the entire universe

> B: it includes both body and mind

> C: it includes both self and environment

> D: it gives rise to good and evil

E: it encompasses cause and effect simultaneously

So far from Wikipedia.

Success takes focus, desire, effort, hard work, determination and perseverance.

Ichinen covers them all and chanting for what you want to achieve makes your Ichinen stronger and stronger.

In this context, it is a good idea to talk about KI

I give you some thoughts about **KI**, the universal power and energy – the source and motor for everything.

The universe supplied each of us with a good boat and strong oars. This boat is our body and we cruise through life with it. To recognize, develop and use all the best which is in our boat, this universal KI power is the key to run someone's life happily and successfully.

And this KI is not only inside us humans. All creatures, even a tree, a blade of grass, a stone, the water and the air lives off and through KI. Everything is therefore a part of this universe, where everything comes from and everything is within.

Our life is part of this universal KI. As we are a part of the universe, we breathe KI and when this connection is working well, we are healthy and happy. When the KI becomes weak, we become slack and if the flow stops > we die!

Well, how to keep the flow running and how to stay happy, successful, healthy and all that? Here, we have to look at the difference between positive and negative. Simply said: If you want to become ill, you will. If not, then not! As easy as that. This is called Yin and Yang.

The symbol of Yin and Yang

Is it really this simple? Yes and no. Of course one has to have a positive attitude towards things. Negative is destructive and harms you. So work on positive things for you, stay with the positive and avoid the negative, as it will suck you into this negative being.

To do something happy or miserable with your life, it is finally a decision to be made by yourself. Whether we choose the positive or the negative path it is in our hands. And be aware, whatever you decide, the positive will attract more positive and so does the negative. In this meaning, there is no bad or good destiny in someone's life. We choose which way we want to go.

But you must go and learn how to develop and keep your KI energy.

And as this little booklet is not about KI, I leave it here now as it is.

Beside KI there is another topic, which needs good attention.

It is called meditation.

Sometimes in life one needs guidance and advice. The following is an extract from a worksheet I did for my students some years ago. I talk about the value of mediation and how it can be approached.

I have been meditating myself for many years now and I still do meditate on a regular basis. This is for me like refuelling regularly. Basically it started for me when I entered the world of the Martial Arts and Yoga. In 1989 when I graduated as a 1st Dan Jiu-Jitsu I was already close to other masters who offered meditation and I was lucky to study and sit with them. In 1996 I spent a lot of time with my Dutch friend Annemijn Jansen from Utrecht/Nederland who was involved in the Birinsi Institute of Yoga and later I graduated with them as a Tantra Yoga teacher. After that I have never been without meditation.

"No matter how you feel. Get up, get to the dojo. You feel better afterwards!" (Wise words by Master Horst)

This is the meditation chamber I created and used when living in Symondsbury/UK in 1993. It was for men only!

I have compiled a selection of the topics I found relevant to know and hope they will raise your interest too.

1. Meditation is not what the people say and what you read about in the media or social media sometimes. Before the meditation there is the concentration and after that the contemplation.

2. You cannot learn meditation from books or other media. You need personal advice, because meditation opens doors

of your life that might give you a struggle to deal with on your own.

3. There are many ways how to meditate. Best is to choose at first one only and stick to it for good progress.

4. You need daily practise! And do not expect fast results.

5. Meditation will change your circumstances (Life) but it is not a quick fix.

6. Keep it simple. A simple approach is good for many things in life.

7. Stay happy along the way. It helps a lot!

8. The fire of emotions needs to be kept low.

9. Patience is the essence of a man says an Asian proverb. Be patient with all what comes.

10. Free your mind from all these stories.

11. At Ichinen we meditate together every Monday morning at 10 am. Join in and start your journey.

Master Horst D. Lindenau practising meditation in the Zen garden

Yoga - What has Yoga to do with the martial arts?

When I studied martial arts at the German based Budo Academy Europe under supervision of late Grand master Horst Weiland (†) I got introduced to Yoga. Grand master Weiland was not only a highly decorated martial artist (I believe he had some 35 master degrees at that time), he was a professor for Yoga as well. After the introduction period at the academy, I decided to study Yoga additionally to the martial arts and since then I have never regretted this wonderful move. I left the academy as a "Yoga-Assistant", which is one degree below the teacher grade in Hatha Yoga. I like to say special thanks to my other Yoga teacher at the academy, Mrs. Lusensky, who was the most graceful woman I ever met. I assume she was in her late 60s and her whole appearance was that like a young girl when she practiced Yoga.

So, what actually is Yoga? I studied Hatha Yoga and Euro-Yoga with

Mr. Weiland and Mrs. Lusensky and I remember asking him once what Yoga is. He stood behind the desk in our Dojo and put a piece of chalk in front of me and said, that's what it is. I still use this answer when people ask me that question today.

There are 100.000s of pages and books written about Yoga, it is probably the oldest system of physical and mental exercises. Yoga is not an art like the martial arts. It is beyond that. The moment you attach the word Yoga, it indicates it is a complete path by itself. The word Yoga means, what brings you to reality; literally, it means union.

There are many ways to approach this magnificent system called Yoga. It branches out to some main disciplines, known as Hatha-, Raja-, Gnani-, Karma-, Bhakti- or Tantra Yoga. People study the popular Iyengar Yoga or even do a modern hot Yoga. There are no limits to what was invented around this word Yoga and what it is used for.

I decided later to concentrate on the Tantric way of Yoga. And this is purely, because practicing Tantra Yoga does not require you to be vegetarian, nor stopping drinking or smoking, which I quite liked in those days. Tantra Yoga leaves any decision with you and when you are ready to do the right thing, it will come to you. You have to decide which path you want to go at the moment. In spring of 1996 I graduated as Tantra Yoga master with the "Birinsi-Association" based in Utrecht/Nederland. And since then I have never stopped practicing my Yoga and it is the most wonderful complement to the Jiu-Jitsu and martial arts in general. I only know of five people they combined Yoga with the martial arts. One of them is my late Grand master Horst Weiland (10th Dan Jiu-Jitsu and Yoga professor).

Incidents that stopped my training - but not my progress

There have been times in my life, when circumstances forced me to stop training martial arts. Although one might think, it is your own choice, but life sometimes takes a different turn as wanted and expected.

During my life as a sea captain my training came to a complete stop. There was just no time to do it. In earlier years as an able body seaman and officer I took advantage of being in other countries and went whenever the chance was offered to visit dojos all over the world. But that was at a time when staff wasn't short and time in ports were long stay. In those days we spent like fourteen days in places like Hong Kong, Yokohama or Singapore.

When my life took another turn and I made a living as a professional in advertising sales and publishing, I did not put my Gi on for several years. But I believe these breaks in someone's martial arts carrier are not unusual and quite common.

What stopped me several times too were serious injuries. I suffered two bike accidents and both left me with first the left and then the right shoulder broken. One doctor said to me I should find myself another job, rather than Jiu-Jitsu coach. I proved them wrong. After a few years of being a "bit handicapped", I think I even became better than before. Although since then I cannot perform single handed push ups anymore. But still did 60 ordinary when I turned 60 a few years ago.

At one point I damaged my knee. I wasn't warmed up enough and instructed an anti Terrorkampf class in Berlin where we trained kicks to the punch bag. I noticed one student doing his kicks a bit wrong and said to him: "Look, that's the way you do it" and gave it a nice Mawashi Geri. That move resulted in a keyhole operation and I suffered a stiff knee for a year or so.

But these things happen to many of us. And with the right attitude, good physio and some rest you overcome it.

What does not happen to many, and that is good so, that one of your best friends gets killed in a robbery and fight. This disaster too place in Africa and left him beheaded. This changed my life again in a drastic way and I decided to keep training again (after another break) and I wanted to specialize in knife fighting, knife defence; which led later to the creation of the BlackCombat system.

After having been a 1st Dan in Jiu-Jitsu for almost 28 years, finally I had to go for the next grade. The world martial arts association MMA based in Germany awarded me the 2nd Dan Jiu-Jitsu through my old Budo friend Grand master Marco Gevatter, 7th Dan Jiu-Jitsu. I can live with it, as it recognizes not only being a first grade for this long, but because I had already educated over 1000 students in these years.

Sometime in 2019 I hope to be graded 3rd Dan Jiu-Jitsu and this time I decided to present my skills in front of the grading panel at the official Dan and Kyu grades in our school. Wish me luck. Mainly I do that, to prove that training in Jiu-Jitsu and martial arts in general keeps you fit even as you get older. It will be a nice present for my 65th birthday and adds to my studies in the anti-aging field.

"Anti-aging and longevity are my vehicle. And the Jiu-Jitsu is the fuel", I often say. As a result of intensive training in Yoga and meditation I brought all this together with my profound life experience and founded the Terrestrial Life Management (TerLiMa) in 2009. Since then this has developed into a source for anti-aging tools and longevity in general. The key element is live up to a minimum of 115 years and I believe the practice of Jiu-Jitsu contributes to my personal physical and mental wellbeing to join this goal.

As this little compendium is called "My way", I would like to give you an outlook on the future. I believe as long one has got ambitious plans and works on them, life is proceeding in a good way. There is only growth or decay. We must make a decision here. It is not wise to leave it to circumstances. And my decision is that I keep my own training up and at the same time I pass my knowledge on to those that come after me. This is the way the martial arts and Budo stays alive in the world.

And this is a very important fact. Why in the world would one start to study such a thing like Jiu-Jitsu in the first place and why would one continue throughout one's life?

The answer lies in the history and of course within you.

Regarding the history one should not forget, that the techniques and skills were not developed for reasons as we find them nowadays. I am thinking of sports and leisure as a motivation. No, Jiu-Jitsu was purely survival. Stay alive by being able to protect yourself in a fight, in an ambush, against repression from the rulers of that time.

Once you managed to develop decent self defence skills, you could stop training and rely on what you knew. But in my case Jiu-Jitsu became more. It became a tool to keep my boat floating in the sea of life. It is not only the self defence, the physical well being, the alertness – no, it is the mental reason behind it. With the rigorous training regime comes inevitably discipline. I have developed courage to stand up for myself. I have learned to see differences in people and became able to give love but as well to deny without regret.

Jiu-Jitsu is for me the same tool as my Yoga represents. And here I am one of the very few martial arts masters, who practice both, Yoga and Budo. I have learnt this from my Grand master Horst Weiland †️ who did the same. He used to practice a system he called Mebethe, the Meditative Motion Therapy. Which is not less than Yoga in movement, or even call it Tai Chi. He was a man far ahead of his time.

As you learned earlier on, I took up the martial arts in the first place when I studied Shotokan Karate. That was clearly and purely for one reason. I wanted to learn self defence. At that time there was no other thought within my engagement.

Later I changed styles to Anti-Terrorkampf (Anti Terror Combat) and Jiu-Jitsu with exactly the same idea on my mind. To improve my self defence skills. Only years later, after I practiced myself as a 1st Dan Jiu-Jitsu and had already a couple of hundred students, a significant change happened to me. I became aware, that the Jiu-Jitsu practice was more than a physical procedure or something to improve self defence only. When I studied the history of the art and when I started to gain an insight into the Japanese mythology, only then a much wider insight opened up to me.

Jiu-Jitsu became a tool to master life in general. Not only in the present, but understand the own past and future too. I learned that one can stay physically and mentally young with these exercises and by following these traditions. Therefore Jiu-Jitsu is one of the columns I built my anti-aging methodology on.

The syllabus you find in this book does not contain any of the spiritual or longevity aspects I mentioned. The novice first learns the art from the self defence approach and it will be mainly physical. The higher ground must be developed later when a good foundation is formed. Although there are seminars available from Ichinen Bridport beside the regular training they supply such content.

The spirit of Ichinen Bridport

These guidelines are very much the same as we find in modern Judo. As Judo can be looked at like a child born from Jiu-Jitsu.

Your training and engagement is shaping you. Therefore have trust in its teaching and if necessary be willing to make sacrifices.

The dojo is the place where you can do so and learn your skills. It shall be an unprofane place for you. Show respect as you show respect to your own house.

Take advice from higher grades and be patient and helpful to lower grades.

Pay respect and greet them well, your teacher and the higher grades.

Pay homage to your teacher and follow his example and be a guide to your comrades.

"Ji Ta Kyo Ei" - "The best for me and the others" shall be the advice when training with equal students.

"Seiry Koku Zenhyo" - "The maximum in physical and moral exertion" shall lead your training as your life.

Care for neat and clean tatami, Gi and your own body. Don't use intensive deodorants or perfumes when training.

Defeat is the same as victory in fighting and shall urge you to perfection. A victory is not a reason for rest.

Act always according to the ethics of Jiu-Jitsu and never void its principles.

Reishiki – Etiquette

Reishiki was developed in Japan to a high degree in the Tokugawa period (Ca. 1600-1850). The great neo Confucian movement of the age was a major impetus, infusing the act with the hierarchical meaning we find today.

So why do we bow to the instructor, our fellow students or entering the dojo when we practice the Japanese martial arts? This behaviour goes right back to Reishiki.

That bowing indicates respect, which is a form of polite action in the dojo. It has nothing to do with any kind of subservience. It is this method of Reishiki, which we inherited from those they brought us the art of Budo.

We bow to our instructor for no other reason than to say thank you. He has worked hard for to achieve the level of skill that can now be passed on to you. That commitment should be appreciated since the work that has gone before makes your learning easier. The bows tell the teacher and the student that one appreciates the effort and respect it enough to give the best effort to learn what you can.

The bows are not a form of submission, but a way of practicing safely and with alertness. Budo begins and ends with Reishiki.

As you enter and leave the dojo you stop, put your feet together and bow toward the practice surface. You pay respect as you enter or leave.

I believe the biggest reason to take up Jiu-Jitsu training is to lose the ego. If you cannot bow to someone else without feeling as if you are submitting somehow to them, then you have no chance of obtaining egolessness.

Reishiki goes beyond simply bowing in the modern dojo, just as it did decades ago. Etiquette defines how you enter and leave the room, how you move past your fellow students, how you sit or stand and how you practice.

If everyone is following the same code of behavior, everyone will know what to expect in a class.

The bow to Shomen performed at the start and end of each class, reflects on the history of our art and style of Jiu-Jitsu. It respects the founder and the previous instructors of the art. At Ichinen we bow at a special poster which represents a Shinto shrine and all what is important for us.

Bow to Sensei at the start and end of a class is another good practice. It expresses your willingness to learn and your request to be instructed. You show your gratitude for the patience and ability of the Sensei. During a class you will have a chance to thank the instructor for advice or correction by bowing.

If you work with a partner, you will bow to each other. Bow carefully and with attention and by doing so it is as you say to your partner please practice with me and thank you for your cooperation.

The way you observe the etiquette of the dojo shows a lot about your attitude towards the art, senior students and your Sensei.

This Reishiki is probably one of the big differences to simple sport martial arts.

When you take part in a session you should be well prepared. Your gear (Gi) is clean and not smelly, so is your body. Finger nails are short and very long hair has to be treated in a way, that it does not destruct from your or your partners training.

Eating is not allowed in a dojo. Drinking plenty of water, when needed is a good advice. Mobile phones have to be switched off.

Jewelry has to be taken off, best to leave it at home. Always report to the Sensei when accessing or leaving the mat.

The real reason

I started years ago martial arts training for the simple reason to protect myself. Many do so as I know from my time as a teacher and many others give this up at some point due to various circumstances. I had breaks myself since then, but always returned to the dojo. I did the typical breaks. First got engaged and had to look after this girl rather than training. Another time I was too busy with earning money and twice I stopped to recover from bike accidents. The misuse of too much alcohol has kept me off the dojo at certain times.

Over the years the reason of personal self defence becomes redundant. You know your stuff and everybody should be warned not to come near you. So why continue?

If one is engaged with one's own martial arts school for example, that gives a pretty good reason to stick to it. There are always dates coming up in the future to look forward to. The school is like having children. Things are developing all the time.

But there is more to it. I recognized that regular Jiu-Jitsu training gives me a guide. It helps me mentally and physically to stay on top of the job. And even in difficult life circumstances it is always a great help and acts like a lighthouse. Guiding my boat through life nice and safely.

Today I have discovered another good reason. It is simple anti-aging and therefore longevity. If one can still do the full range of techniques such as rolling, throwing and being thrown, randori and power warm up at the age of 64, there must be something more than pure self defence and jumping about. It is the Jiu-Jitsu Do. It is the way with Jiu-Jitsu.

Martial artist of the month

Each month one member at Ichinen Bridport becomes selected as the martial artist of the month. This fine tradition goes back to 2015, when one of the Jiu-Jitsu students attending training twice the week regularly despite the fact, he had to go straight to his night shift work after training. He got a new girl friend and finally quit the training…

Others qualified for being the only child and training up to yellow belt just with adult partners. And he did very well coping with them all those much larger and older training partners and stood his ground in self defence tests against all individual. Great job!

One little girl was awarded to be the youngest in the group and never missed a single session! Others got this award for attending most hours at the dojo and doing the fastest progress in studies or reached 400 hours of Jiu-Jitsu training. May there be loads more and become a good example for others within the club and beyond.

Since then we had nineteen members who got this precious honour. It needs a special recognition, that's why there isn't an award some months.

When you slow down and stop training -

Get your Gi on and go to the dojo!

A black belt is only the sum of hundreds of classes, not due to a special talent. Losing momentum is the cause of many failed hobbies, talents, dreams and projects. In trying to get any goal accomplished, one forgets that this is made of a thousand little steps. You don't have to do amazing feats. You just have to go to your class regular.

There are as many reasons to halt as there are students. Each has his own personal faith. It says, that within all of the martial arts only a very few actually get to the goal and become at least a 1st Dan black belt. There must be something very special about this black belt, as in comparison to university courses where most finish with 50% or even a higher number of graduates.

In martial arts, after years of dedicated training, the enthusiasm begins to slow down. Sometimes, it just stops suddenly but for the instructor, no student slips away unnoticed. (Should!)

When the student starts showing up less or even stops abrupt to attend, there are many reasons why this happens. Money must be earned, family requires an investment of quality time, and for many teenagers, just getting to the dojo relies on parental availability and willingness. Mind you, in the old days we used to go by bus or cycle. Injuries can cause an unwanted break which becomes a longer abstinence. In my personal case once it was the new fiancée which stopped me going. Silly me!

A missed class can easily become two. Two classes becomes a month. And so on.

But hey, keep in mind! You can always go back. The Sensei and any other students will be delighted to see you return. All that matters is that you make the decision to put your Gi on and get to the dojo. And just in case you are thinking about the excuse, that you are not fit enough anymore; so few people are genuinely fit when they start in the first place. Fitness will come back faster than you think, and honestly? It's not that important.

My maxima is, never miss training. Only exception is your mother's funeral. OK, this is a bit drastic, but we do traditional Japanese Jiu-Jitsu and there is little room for being weak.

If you have a virus, stay out the dojo. If you have an exam tomorrow, still show up, as it will do you good. In case of injury or light illness, always attend and sit and watch.

Health benefits of practising Jiu-Jitsu

Talking benefits, there are health risks too of course. I will talk about that later on. As in any physical activity either work or sports, there is always a risk to your health involved by doing it wrong or too excessive. The consideration of not doing anything is not the answer. First we want to train Jiu-Jitsu and everyone knows very well, that not doing any physical activity leads to decay pretty soon.

Beside the physical health benefits of practicing Jiu-Jitsu, there is a huge mental factor, which is important. Better self confidence, good mood, balanced life style, no drug and alcohol abuse and a clear mind are just a few to be mentioned.

The regular training of Jiu-Jitsu will give you excellent coordination, an improved reaction time, definitely greater endurance and growth in strength and flexibility. You will develop a good speed and become more flexible in your reactions. Balance, both dynamic and static will be very good.

Longevity and Jiu-Jitsu

The regular training of Jiu-Jitsu has got a positive effect on longevity and acts like an anti-aging tool. This martial art can only be highly recommended. This special way of training Jiu-Jitsu encloses the entire body and mind.

No nation in the world is getting older than the Japanese. Over 23.000 Japanese are over 100 years old today. Whether this is a contribution to their lifestyle, genes, religion, nutrition, environment or even the fact that so many of them practice the Japanese Budo styles? We don't know. Fact is, spirituality holds the soul - and the body a few more years.

It says: "When the mind is sitting, then the body is also sitting" (Buddhist wisdom).

Fish is the staple food in Japan alongside rice and the main beverage is tea, green tea! Japanese swear by their green tea.

It says: "Peace is in a cup of tea" (Buddhist wisdom).

For most Japanese, green tea might be the main cause of their high life expectancy. They believe that it protects them from cancer, tooth decay, high blood pressure, stroke and arteriosclerosis, keeps them slim, controls blood sugar levels, strengthens capillaries and detoxifies the body during radioactive rainfall. But it's still nice to believe that Japanese Jiu-Jitsu might be another reason for a long life.

If we look deeper into the biology of strength training, we find that the critical point is to combine the various approaches a particular exercise does for the body. Strength training causes the muscle growth. Aerobic training is good for endurance.

What is missing is the perfect coordination of the body and mind. Only the well balanced coordination within the exercise improves the longevity effect. And I am not talking of the coordination of hand and eyes, but the fine muscle system which links your body with the brain and vice versa. Join a good Jiu-Jitsu school near you and fight the decay. Jiu-Jitsu is suitable for any age and it will keep you young in all aspects.

Within my life coaching system there is an item called Club 115. This stands for people who aim to become 115 years old! This Club 115 supports its members to live meaningful and healthy up to 115 years. Club 115 is part of my long years work on longevity and anti-aging which I began already in 2005. I understand my involvement for the martial arts, my own physical and mental training of the arts as a fountain of youth. Jiu-Jitsu keeps me fit, supple and alert.

Risks of accidents and injuries

Jiu-Jitsu and the martial arts in general are listed as medium risks with insurers. Here we play in the same league as e.g. badminton or riding a bike. Football, Handball, Rugby or skiing are far more risky and severe injuries happen more often. Within the martial arts the Jiu-Jitsu is at the safer end regarding accidents. Sure MMA with cage fighting and boxing are found at the top of the high risk level list.

To avoid accidents, it is important that the instructor gives the very best advice to students when sparring, practicing randori and training with a partner regular techniques. Both, Uke and Tori have to care for each other and this works best in a respectful and well supervised dojo.

Special care has to be taken by handling weapons, training several attackers scenarios, exercising outdoors or with the lights switched off.

The insurer provides you with a list of things that are covered during training and to stay on the safe side, this has to be strictly followed.

To avoid injury in any sport, it is important to have a warm up period before one goes into hard core action. That helps a lot. Further it is necessary to stick to the rules. We had an accident once during randori on the floor only and it was the order not to stand up. Of course someone always tries to be clever and ignore the rules. Well he broke his arm during that action.

But it is not only someone's own fault to get injured. As in the world of work, where most accidents to an individual are caused by others like workmates etc. it can be similar in the martial arts. Before we interact and train with a partner, we bow to each other. This means without words "you can trust me, I respect you, I stick to the rules, I will learn together with you" or similar phrases.

But here too are some characters, that cannot do so. I had a student who was a brown belt in Judo already and he always bullied and hurt his training partners as soon I was not watching. When training with me he never behaved badly. Only after he lightly injured a yellow belt and others spoke out about it could I question him and finally suspended him from class as he was not able to learn.

When living in France for a couple of years, I attended a local KungFu school in the town of Bordeaux. What a wonderful place that was, very good Sifu and I was happy to continue my studies in this style. One day I was sparring with someone, who didn't like the idea of a German Jiu-Jitsu black belt attending "his" KungFu. During sparring he smashed his fist into my teeth and for a moment I thought, ok that's three grand for denture. I was lucky, just the lip split and no teeth out.

It is very often the attitude of some martial artists, they either need to bully and hurt others deliberately by nature, due to their bad character or have an ego which doesn't allow them any mercy or care for others. Luckily in our local Ichinen School and in all my 30 years of teaching, I had just two accidents to report to the insurance company. As an instructor you have to sort the rotten apples out before they do harm to the others. At Ichinen Bridport we are ruthless with people who don't fit in and play by the rules as everybody else.

Of course sometimes it does not need anybody else to get injured.

During a 2nd Dan grading in the style of Anti-Terrorkampf I did a breaking test and after the grading I had to attend A&E. The knuckles of my right hand were severely damaged. The surgeon threatened me with no treatment as he thought this was self inflicted and rather stupid to break bricks with your hand. Maybe there is some truth in it but on the other hand, we need a tough training and I believe, there is no black belt holder who hasn't had any injuries during his way towards 1st Dan. In Shotokan Karate they used to say: "A black belt has broken all of his eleven toes".

Thinking toes, they are actually the most vulnerable parts to get damaged. That is why in our Jiu-Jitsu style we wear leather boots as in wrestling. This and the fact, that the modern zigzag mats haven't got these vicious gaps anymore, injuries on the feet are very rare today.

Still some parts of the body can cause trouble. I mention shoulders, ribs, knees and sometimes the fingers. But if you stick to the rules and keep your mind clear the training of Jiu-Jitsu and most other martial arts is not classified as dangerous and therefore we pay very little insurance here in the UK.

Some advice for the student

Don't think that one training per week that you attend will make or keep you fit. Fit enough to challenge the aim you have set yourself. To become a martial artist, a warrior, a fighter in life, you will have to master the discipline.

Therefore you can do the following:

Make sure you attend at each single lesson. Give yourself the discipline to do so. There is only one reason not to come to the class, when your mother dies! I gave up martial arts training during my way through life for certain reasons several times. And I regret it! Reasons like, a new fiancée, work, interest in other things and as well of course too lazy! Unfortunately I did not have the master to tell me what I tell you now.

Establish a daily routine with some kind of exercise. I change between press ups, sit-ups, chin-ups, running, cycling and swimming. Even walking is fine, especially if you have a job where you sit most of the time.

Do breathing methods. More information about that you can find on our blog http://jiu-jitsuinbridport.blogspot.com/ and there are lots of good books available and we learn it too in the class. Or join the meditation group at Ichinen Bridport which is excellent to learn not only the right way of breathing but meditation too.

My biggest idol, KungFu Master Bruce Lee † said: "Jogging is the best method to become and stay fit." Do it. It doesn't cost anything.

If you cannot join the class activity due to illness or other reasons, turn up anyway and watch. First you don't break your weekly routine by having a clear commitment. Second you will find out that just watching the class is very beneficial too. Make notes, maybe take some pictures, observe your comrades doing similar techniques. Stay in touch!

If you can't do the odd training night because you are busy that day, go and do an hour jogging instead another day of the week or even visit some other martial arts which is on offer in your town.

Does Jiu-Jitsu incorporate the Kiai?

This loud shout we know from other martial arts as in Karate and Taekwondo you'll find as well in our Jiu-Jitsu practice. A short yell used by executing a technique to perform strongest. A Kiai can be used in a self defence situation as destruction or even as an audible attack.

The dynamics of a Kiai come from proper use of the breathing. The good coordination of breathing and moving is essential.

The benefits to practice and use a Kiai are numerous. It prepares the body mentally and physically as the level of adrenalin will increase. It gives bigger strength and power by striking and kicking and your own body gets protected like having a shield when execute the Kiai.

Jiu-Jitsu and self defence

At Ichinen Bridport we train Jiu-Jitsu for personal growth (mental and physical) as well as for self defence. Everyone who becomes a green belt (3rd Kyu) within our school must be able to defend him/herself against common bullying and violent situations.

The syllabus contains the training against the most common attacks regarding to law enforcement in the UK from 2017 and on top of that we make use of all sorts of weapons which can be useful for self protection. Of course this does not mean, that a green belt level enables you to stand in a terror like street attack of criminals who have no mercy and respect of anybody's life. It means that you should be able to handle ordinary situations of violent behavior and as you continue studying Jiu-Jitsu your skills will increase.

There is a big difference between pub brawls, domestic fight and a punch up in a school yard against utmost violence executed by human monsters, street gangs and nasty criminals. To face this kind of challenge it needs more than once a week Jiu-Jitsu training to be honest. Therefore we teach on top of the Jiu-Jitsu in our school the modern style of BlackCombat self defence, which is the successor of Anti Terror Combat.

"If the fight isn't over in a Blitz you might lose it." (Wise words by Master Horst)

We all know this story, when the little boy comes home crying and dad asks him, if he didn't use his BJJ skills for defence? "Yes," says the boy in tears, "but when I tapped he didn't stop hitting me!" That describes best the difference between sport BJJ and traditional Jiu-Jitsu like ours which focuses strongly on real self defence.

In a competition fight there are rules. And in a competition there is the referee. And there is light. It is warm. The attacker is same age, same sex, and same weight and even wears same uniform. On the street the thug is looking for his pray. And he picks the easy one. It is unexpected, violent, unfair, brutal and quick. If you are not prepared you'll get your bash. It is an important fact to make a difference within the various martial arts and Jiu-Jitsu styles. They all have their good reasons and they all are good in various fields. The Jiu-Jitsu we learn is with a big focus on self defence. And always keep in mind: "The biggest enemy is you yourself!"

These are the pillars of Jiu-Jitsu

This is my very personal advice about rules and principles of Jiu-Jitsu.

1   change > change > change!

> work fluently; go from one application to the next until you succeed.

2   You always can change your own location.

> By repositioning you gain advantage.

3   Don't try to apply "10% more power/strength "in a technique which fails. It does not work.

> have an alternative technique.

4   When grabbing always use 100% strength.

5   When striking the minimum should be three times. Produce a firework of blows.

6   Observation of eyes/view. Where is the attacker looking at?

     > watch the attackers shoulders.

7   Upstairs/downstairs

     > Lower attack, higher attack, and lower attack.

8   Keep your hands up. Keep a guard up.

9   Maintain enough distance to give yourself time to muster a counterattack.

And this is my very personal advice for you for self defence

Some ideas are found within the BlackCombat system. Finally it all goes back to the "mother of the art – Jiu-Jitsu".

https://www.blackcombat.org/

It does little good to learn defensive techniques to counter moves that your opponent may never launch. Know how a criminal on the street attacks, how a mentally ill or drugged person attacks, how a rapist attacks and so on. Seek that information from people who've been there. Don't believe those "sport and event only masters" when it comes to dangerous self defence situations!

Become familiar with being struck; become familiar with being hit hard. Condition yourself through drilling with a medicine ball or a car tyre, striking a makiwara and engaging in impact sparring with kicks, punches and grappling manoeuvres. And don't do these all padded up trainings. On the street you won't have any of this fancy equipment.

Technique, fitness, long term knowledge and training in combat and philosophy are the qualities that differentiate you from an ordinary street fighter or mugger and give you superiority and safety.

Knowledge is a powerful thing. The more knowledge you have the better martial artist you are. Cross train to learn the strengths and advantages of other styles.

You might be able to do a certain technique with ease every time in a safe environment as your dojo and then completely fail on the street in an unfamiliar environment. That's why it is important to train in self defence on special occasions and seminars in various places such as outdoors, furnished room, work spaces, in cars and so on.

Never underestimate any foe. A physically big attacker can be less challenging than some small guys. Size does not matter!

Be in control at all times. There's no room for anger, fear or doubt. Therefore mind control needs to be part of your Jiu-Jitsu training. This is one reason we cooperate meditation in our training.

If you can knock out a guy with one strike and the fight is over, perfect. But if the guy is bigger and stronger and can absorb your punch … That's why you need certain special skills for the nasty street fight as for example trained in BlackCombat. Which is nothing else than a compilation of very effective self defence Jiu-Jitsu skills.

At Ichinen Bridport we use these techniques for self defence. These are forbidden in MMA matches, so we know they are effective.

These are some techniques that are forbidden in UFC fights/MMA

1.   Head butt

2.   Eyes gouging

3.   Biting

4.   Hair pulling

5.   Fish hooking

6.   Groin attacks

7.   Small joint manipulation

8.   Strike to spine

9.   Throat strikes

10.   Clawing, pinching the flesh

11.   Grab clavicle

12.   Kneeing the head when grounded

13.   Kicking kidneys

14.   Spitting

15.   Abusive language / Kiai

16.   Faking an injury

If you are an instructor, keep in mind that the insurance might not cover you when training these skills. This should not stop you from practicing them, as long you have good safety rules in place and everybody is aware of them.

Very important is the training with weapons when it comes to self defence. I give you a list of training weapons we use in our school. There are two kinds, natural and unnatural weapons.

What is a weapon?

A definition found on Wikipedia:

"A weapon, arm, or armament is any device used in order to inflict damage or harm to living beings, structures, or systems. Weapons are used to increase the efficacy and efficiency of activities such as hunting, crime, law enforcement, self defence, and warfare. In a broader context, weapons may be construed to include anything used to gain a strategic, material or mental advantage over an adversary.

While ordinary objects such as sticks, stones, cars, or pencils can be used as weapons, many are expressly designed for the purpose – ranging from simple implements such as clubs to swords and guns."

So far what Wikipedia has to tell us about it.

Some samples for "ordinary weapons"

Short stick - Long stick – Tonfa – Handgun - Knife, any bladed weapons - Baseball bat, clubs – Axe

Samples for „daily life weapons"

Stone – Ashtray – Chair – Shoe - Glass, any cup - Bottle – Firelighter – Mobile phone – Scissors – Needles – Cutlery – Book – Magazine – Shoe - Razor blade - Dog

Read this before you intend to handle or use or even carry any weapon:

http://www.cps.gov.uk/legal/l_to_o/offensive_weapons_knives_bla ded_and_pointed_articles/

http://www.cps.gov.uk/legal/s_to_u/sentencing_manual/knives_an d_offensive_weapons/

http://www.thesite.org/homelawandmoney/law/weaponscrime/wea ponsandthelaw

Links in a printed medium might not function after certain time. In this case, just Google.

The very best weapon of all does not need to be listed.

It's you!

Talking about weapons I like to remember my late friend master Trevor Barton. Trevor was a member of Ichinen Bridport until his sudden death in 2017. Before he joined us he studied Taekwondo and Karate. In Jiu-Jitsu he graduated up the 3rd Kyu but his most interest he found in practicing Anti Terror Combat (Today BlackCombat). In this system Trevor was a 1st Dan black belt and until his death he was the weapon officer and responsible for the development of weapon skills. Master Trevor left us a detailed guide for self defence on transport. Trevor you are deeply missed. Oss!

(See front cover: Master Horst congratulates Trevor Barton to his 3rd Kyu Jiu-Jitsu 2107)

Weapons for self defence training at Ichinen Bridport

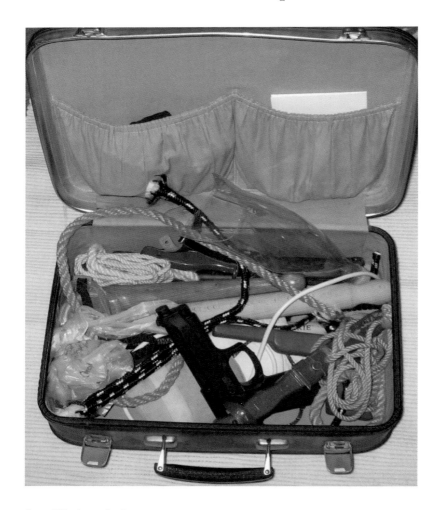

1. Various knives
2. Hammer
3. Ashtray
4. Broken bottle
5. Screw driver
6. Scissors
7. Short stick

8. Pistol
9. Axe
10. Cable
11. Rope
12. Walking stick / umbrella
13. Knuckle duster
14. Small battery, fire lighter, coin, small stone, cork
15. Carrier bag
16. Rolled up magazine
17. Long stick
18. Base bat
19. Pepper spray (illegal in the UK)
20. Kubotan (illegal in the UK)
21. Tonfa (illegal in the UK)

*** Always keep on mind: observe the weapon laws, don't break the law! At time of printing the sentence in the UK for carrying a knife in public was four years in prison!

The weapons to train self defence have to reflect the real threat on the streets in our modern world. I appreciate it if martial artists train with some ancient Japanese weapons, but they don't prepare that much for the real attacks today, if that is all what they use in training.

Traditional weapons are often used for the mind work. To perform Kata, study various moves and connect the user with the old traditions. This is important too and cannot be neglected.

The ten most common (street) attacks according to law enforcement (2015/UK)

At Ichinen Bridport we say, "we do not want to invent the wheel new", therefore the following listing of common attacks will be the first set we concentrate on. This is based on information supplied by government law enforcement. I will set up scenarios for you that mirror the top ten street attacks. Students will be taught to understand the dynamics of the situation as well as the techniques that can be used to deal with them. As everything is continuously changing, there will be a summary of techniques in future work sheets to update with the latest developments. And most importantly, our syllabus for all future belt grading will be revised and changed to the new knowledge according to circumstances. We don't do same old same old.

Ichinen Bridport is the only martial arts school in South West Dorset, which has got the ten most common street attacks according to law enforcement in their grading syllabus. The complete list of these common attacks includes over one hundred dangerous, nasty and surprising situations, which we cover randomly too.

To concentrate on these real street defence scenarios makes all the difference in some ones chances to react in a distressful situation successfully and effectively. Students train constantly on the ten most common street attacks.

The evolution of violence and disorder in public areas is constant changing and our instructors have close contact to what really matters in real street defence. I have worked as a certified security officer myself and can pass on my experience to the students.

The ten most common attacks according to law enforcement

1. One person pushes, hands to chest, which is normally followed by the pusher striking first, to the head.

2. A swinging punch to the head.

3. A front clothing grab, one handed, followed by a punch to the head.

4. A front clothing grab, two hands, followed by a head butt.

5. A front clothing grab, two hands, followed by a knee to the groin.

6. A bottle, glass, or ashtray to the head.

7. A lashing kick to the groin or lower legs.

8. A broken bottle or glass jabbed to face.

9. A slash with a knife, most commonly a 3 to 4" lock blade knife or kitchen utility knife.

10. A grappling style head lock.

Before any self defence situation occurs, there will be various signs which have to be identified and assessed. Very much as in other situations like an accident or a complex work task.

You have to think about the situation first, before you take up any action. Questions are, how serious is the threat? What kind of opponent, just one or any others? Are there any weapons involved? Can I escape before any violence starts? Can I cope at this present moment on my own? Is it advisable to do a pre-emptive strike?

As better the self defence training and preparation you had in the past, as quicker and safer you can answer these questions..

It's all about assessing the situation and make the right decisions.

And all these decisions have to be made often in a split second. As better one is prepared and act out of subconsciousness, as better the outcome and the chance to stay safe.

This "checklist" needs to be in your subconsciousness.

- Is this a dangerous situation for me or others?

- What about the offender? What kind? Type?

- Are more than two people at the scene?

- What about weapons?

- CCTV cameras around?

- Is it domestic or public?

- Escape possible before and after the confrontation?

- Am I ready for defence action?

- Any unnatural weapons available? As well for the offender!

Jiu-Jitsu is very useful as self defence

As we train Jiu-Jitsu with a big focus on self defence, I cannot think of a better style to support your future self defence. The reason I say so is based on the knowledge that Jiu-Jitsu is really flexible and adaptive for any practitioner, never mind what age or sex.

Jiu-Jitsu training covers all situations they might occur when needed in a stressful self defence situation. It covers all common attacks and deals with armed and unarmed offenders. As the training is done on soft mats, profound ground work is included. Before you decide to join any self defence class you should consider certain points.

- Is there an insurance cover with the course?

- Is the instructor knowledgeable in the world of real street fights?

- Are training mats available?

- Make sure you don't attend a course which is overcrowded.

- Has the instructor serious qualifications, DBS check and 1st aid training?

- Is the level of tuition suitable for you?

- Does the course handle the psychology of self defence, like anti bullying strategies, fear management and self confidence?

- Is the course flexible in its teachings or is it based on just one style, which might exclude various techniques?

- Does the course deal with the most common attacks?

- Does the course include training against armed attackers?

Other styles

I remember well, when one of my long term students marched out of the dojo, after I told him, as long I am the sensei here, BJJ is not coming over this threshold. Today I still laugh about it. It was more an exercise and experience for both of us. I should have been more patient and thoughtful, as I am the master and he, forgive him, should have controlled his ego. This is done and dusted now, as students come – and students go.

But let us look at this BJJ, Brazilian Jiu-Jitsu. First I must say, if one trains a certain style lifelong, which is the traditional Japanese style of Jiu-Jitsu (In my case of course this comes with a strong German touch and impact in it, as my Grand master was German) for me, it will become part of your nature. You cannot avoid to be good at it, regardless of the style. Then it is rather normal to stick with what you have got and what you know, what became your individual tradition.

And this BJJ is nothing else than another offspring from the Japanese source of our art, only well promoted in this modern world of internet and media. It is a bit the Americanization of this art. And although I except it is every persons individual decision, it's not my cup of tea.

Technically I stick to what the old masters said: A mountain does not criticize the river for not being as high and the river does not criticize the mountain for not having any water. Full stop.

I don't prefer BJJ as it is too much of a sport rather than self defence and that is what I focus on.

Oh, and when this student walked out I told him too that MMA does not enter the dojo either. Well, mixed martial arts is another American sport which is good for some but best for money and entertainment. I stick to the traditional view.

And don't take me wrong. I did and I still do train many different styles. This is important to be and stay a good teacher for my students. But I tell you, I like to make a difference between what is suitable and what is nonsense. And there is a lot of useless stuff out there. I have trained many styles in the past and I am always open for new experiences and influence on our training. When I stop to learn myself from other arts, which is probably the moment I am close to death myself.

Shotokan Karate was my absolute favorite for years and if life would have led me other paths, I would teach that art today. And when I find the time I will continue my Kung Fu training and master it. There is always something to do.

Master Horst D. Lindenau in his first own Dojo, SDS Bremen 1989

Judo is essential to know about and to study. It can help a lot to perform better in any Jiu-Jitsu style.

And here comes the question, what do we call our art? In Japanese Jiu-Jitsu has got its own character. In the translation to the western languages it can turn out as Ju Jutsu, Jiu Jitsu, Jujitsu and even BJJ and many more. It has to do with dialect, historical transmission and last but not least what reached us and got established.

Even the styles with the same kind of writing as Jiu-Jitsu can vary a lot. Some concentrate on self defence, others on sport and competitions.

In Germany I trained for a while All style Do Karate within the Budo Akademie Europa. This is more a westernized approach to Japanese Karate and rather a self defence than a "Do". It depends on your master what he focuses on.

As well in the Budo Akademie Europa (BAE) there was Ajukate which I trained too and gained the 1st Kyu. A=Aikido, Ju=Judo and Jiu-Jitsu, K=Karate and Te stands for Terror Combat. This is the all style system of that organization.

If I would have the time and the room in my life, I would continue with the studies of Kung Fu as mentioned before. My first teacher was a young Turk in Germany. His name was Hakam and he taught me the basics of this wonderful art. Since then it is one of my number one choices of styles. I continued Kung Fu when I lived in Bordeaux / France. Ok, that's past now.

And mind you, famous Bruce Lee is my most precious martial artist I respect and honor. He was and still is a very big influence.

More styles? Yes, there are about 30.000 martial arts organizations all over the world today and they have all their different ways. And that is good so.

In 1996 I started to develop a pagan style martial art together with my friend Uwe Ecker, the head of the Berlin pagans in Germany at that time. We made quite good progress with it. Unfortunately his fiancée had an accident and caught fire which brought the development to a halt. So him and me never graduated higher than "Krieger" (warrior).

My next venture was to establish a self defence element within the TerLiMa (Terrestrial Life Management). TerLiMa is a platform and source of knowledge to live a fulfilled life and self defence is one part of the content. I compiled easy to learn and effective self defence skills for the average user.

The final essence of these long years of studying Jiu-Jitsu and other martial arts related subjects lead to the founding of the BlackCombat self defence system. I am the founder and president of this world wide BlackCombat organization which I initiated as a real and purely self defence style.

Jiu-Jitsu and the law

"The answer has to be reasonable"

"You must take no action which would escalate the level of violence"

The guy was in a lift when a thug entered it and asked him to hand over his wristwatch.

Scenario 1: He hands his watch over, the thug left and all done. Except the watch is gone.

Scenario 2: He used a pretty good combat technique. Knocked the thug out and handed him over to the security at the basement. An ambulance took him away. Police arrived at the scene and arrested the defender temporarily.

Months later at court the judge ruled out his sentence. "As you are a black belt in combat fighting, you should have known better. Only to protect you from the loss of a £ 100 worth watch, the victim (!) lost most of his front teeth. He was unemployed already; now he will find it even harder to get a new job. You have to pay full compensation for him and you get sentenced for doing bodily harm to a far weaker opponent."

I heard this story first in 1975 and since the internet is around there are various versions available. They all point out that **"the answer has to be reasonable"**.

You must, wherever possible, try to withdraw, even if this means giving over money or any property.

The good news about this story is, with Jiu-Jitsu you are able to tune your defence according to the situation. You don't need to necessarily punch someone's front teeth or kick him in the groin. There are plenty of defence techniques which work well but don't affect the attacker in a way that he needs A&E treatment next.

As better you are trained, as more perfectly you can react in a violent situation. Laws vary from country to country and so does the level of violence.

What do you think?

Well, in reality a properly educated martial artist, is regarded as an "offensive weapon", same as the fists of a professional boxer. I have been once in a conflict with the law myself, where the judge asked me, if I run a Karate school. Just to find out if I had overdone the self defence bit and can be charged for unreasonable response to an assault. I could answer that question with a "no", as I was running a Jiu-Jitsu school.

You have to be aware, that today nearly every violent conflict between people ends up in front of a court. And as the baddie is often quite used to court cases and police investigation, they have an advantage. And the properly skilled martial artist can be easy blamed for overreaction and his self defence can be classified as inappropriate.

What does that mean for us?

As we all get better and more effective with our skills in combat and fighting every time we attend the training, the chance to be held responsible for the outcome, in case we use some of the skills, is getting bigger with every grade. On the other hand as higher one is qualified, as more professional the reaction can be.

As we don't live with the law of the jungle, we have to obey the law of the land. But before you become disappointed now and start thinking; why shall I learn self defence in the first place? Let me tell you something. It is not about ones wristwatch or a black eye. It is about privilege, ego and self-confidence. And when you are able to control all this inside yourself, you are on the right path.

In 2015 the British government announced a mandatory "two strikes and you're out" minimum six-month prison sentence for carrying a knife. While this obviously does not stop the bad guys to carry a knife and to use it, as we know now in 2019, it gives us clear instruction not to do so ourselves. Never carry a knife, or any other offensive weapon for self defence. It is illegal! And if you know your Jiu-Jitsu skills you don't need any extra weapons.

Of course you can defend yourself without illegal weapons. But keep on mind; **it has to be within the principle of proportionality.** Then you are on the safe side. And one last advice: If you're in a fight and even if you win and the attacker can escape, better go to the police and report the incident firstly yourself. Keep in charge! And keep in training!

And my very personal view of this topic. I am not a lawyer; I do self defence. And if someone attacks me I first think about my safety and good health and my own life. Maybe second about the law. If one assumes to get badly hurt or even killed, it is covered by the law to defend yourself.

And a good advice: Don't break the law of the country you're in!

Note: Whilst every effort has been made to ensure that the advice given in this book is as accurate as possible, the author or the publishers cannot take any responsibility for any injury or loss sustained as a result of the use of this content.

For the latest on law and self defence in the UK you can visit:

https://www.gov.uk/browse/justice

Special about knives:

https://www.gov.uk/buying-carrying-knives

For professionals in England and Wales I recommend a book by martial arts and self-defence authority Leigh Simms LLB (Hons) / 4th Dan. He gives the reader a practical guide in his book "UK self-defence law". But keep in mind, the law might be different in the country where you live and any advice in a printed book could be obsolete after the book has been published.

Anatomy

I once ran a seminar in my German school SDS Bremen with the working title "Anatomy" and it was shattering how little everyone knew about our body. I call the body "boat", as it is the one who sails us through life.

Would you join a boat on a far distant voyage not knowing this boat is fit for purpose? No, of course you wouldn't. But obviously when it comes to our own boat, the body, the attention is often poor.

As a martial artist you need to know your anatomy. You want to know how these joints work; you are going to work on. And you need to be sure; you strike and kick the right points when it comes to a fight. And last but not least it is useful to know some anatomy in case one suffers an injury during training or even in a fight.

We are not after the same level of knowledge as a paramedic or even a doctor, but it is important to have the essentials right.

The human skeleton

The adult human body has 206 bones altogether. We have 28 skull bones, 26 vertebrae (7 cervical or neck, 12 thorax, 5 lumbar or loins, the sacrum which is five fused vertebrae, and the coccyx, our vestigial tail, which is four fused vertebrae.

Then there are 24 ribs plus the sternum or breastbone. The shoulder girdle (2 clavicles, the most frequently fractured bone in the body, and 2 scapulae). The pelvic girdle (2 fused bones). 30 bones are in our arms and legs.

Demonstrating the skeleton here is simply to raise your attention and interest for the anatomy in the human body. As this is not a biology or medicine work, it would be to cursory and I am not qualified enough to give the best insight. All that I know is the fact, that we need to study the anatomy as we deal with the body very closely and intensively and besides that I believe this kind of knowledge is a priority, as your body is like your boat you sail through life.

I was undecided to show this skeleton or rather a map of the veins and arteries which form an incredible network of 80.000 kilometers in length all together. I recommend you go to the library and get a good book about these subjects.

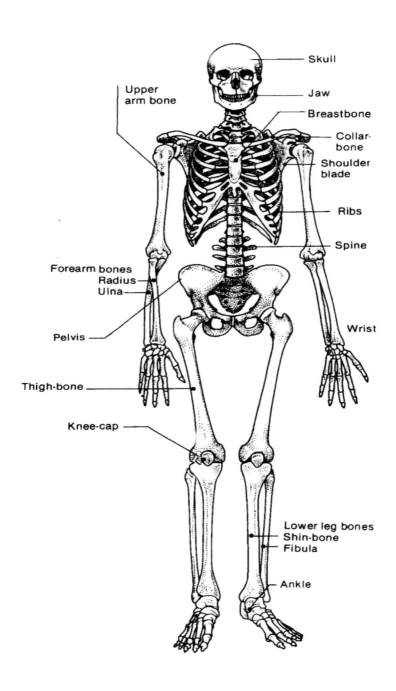

Skull

Jaw

Upper
arm bone

Breastbone

Collar-
bone

Shoulder
blade

Ribs

Spine

Forearm bones
Radius
Ulna

Pelvis

Wrist

Thigh-bone

Knee-cap

Lower leg bones
Shin-bone
Fibula

Ankle

Special Ichinen Bridport work sheets

In my local school Ichinen Bridport I supply the students with regular work sheets. This collection of work sheets gives the students useful information about their training. Jiu-Jitsu, martial arts in general, meditation, yoga and some general life coaching will be covered. The content helps the student to gain some theoretical knowledge which is useful together with the practical training in the dojo to achieve the purpose to reach black belt level one day.

The scholar collects the work sheets as they are published and given free with a full membership at Ichinen Bridport.

This includes some addresses if you need any more information about the work sheets or the Club Ichinen Bridport and the Martial Arts.

Master Horst Lindenau, 86 North Allington, Bridport, DT6 5DZ, phone UK 07968 235486

IMASA / UK are the present governing body. They provide insurance and recognize the grading.

http://www.independentmartialartsportsassociation.co.uk/   phone UK 01246 452878

The web blog of Ichinen Bridport:

https://jiu-jitsuinbridport.blogspot.com/

The web page of Ichinen Bridport:

https://ichinenbridport.com/

And of course, in modern times you find Ichinen Bridport on Facebook too.

https://www.facebook.com/Ichinenbridport/

Here is a warning included. Although both Ichinen Bridport and the author of the specific pages of these work sheets have taken great care to ensure the authentic of the information and techniques published herein, we are not responsible, in whole or in part, for any injury which may occur to the reader by following any instructions given on these work sheets.

We also do not guarantee that the techniques described on these work sheets will be safe and effective in a self defence situation. It is understood that there is a potential for injury when using or demonstrating the techniques herein described. It is essential that the reader who follows any of the described techniques should seek medical advice to ensure he/she is fit to do so and understands the risk of a possible injury. Also, national law and local laws may prohibit the use or possession of weapons described herein.

So far I published 85 worksheets and handed them out to my students at Ichinen Bridport.

The subjects vary from technical issues and the syllabus of Jiu-Jitsu, anatomies and first aid, history of the martial arts and many more. Just to mention a few:

How to use the worksheets

Beginner techniques

Safety tips

10 most common attacks

Self defence topics

Punctuality

What is a weapon?

Law and the martial arts

Weapons for self defence

Meaning of life

What makes one violent?

The structure of Ichinen Bridport

Meditation

Dojo etiquette

Ki

Judo throws

Assisted school support

Don't get bullied

These work sheets assist the students learning. They offer a wide range and depending on the grade of the student, the content prepares for the next step in grading. Training of Jiu-Jitsu is not limited to the practical time in the dojo. As further one climbs up the ladder it is necessary to have a profound theoretical knowledge too.

Meditation

There are various ways to find out about meditation.

The way is either in training or studying with books and social media.

Of course the second choice will make you an expert of the subject. But you will never know what you are talking about.

A grandmother sits for hours knitting in her rocking chair in front of the fire. That is meditation too.

An old fisherman sits for hours in a cafe at the harbour entrance and watches the boats. That is meditation too.

As you are not a grandmother and not quite retired as the fisherman, you want to know where to start, how to start with mediation.

To keep a long story short, what you need first is >

Concentration

After you gained a good level of concentration, you will be able to find a teacher to walk with you for a while and teaching you some basics of meditation practice.

I would strongly recommend not trying to learn mediation by books and social media only. Why? Simple because it does not work.

To make the relation visible between mediation (that's what you asked for) and the way towards it, it is probably somewhere between 1 and 1000. So do not expect any quick results after start.

Best way to start is, just sit down on the floor. Use a pillow for comfort and just sit still for a certain length of time. Do that regular and don't bother or worry about what's in your mind. You need to establish the good practice first before expecting any gain.

Attention: Do not sit on a chair! You might fall asleep and fall down.

Attention: Never use any candles! There is a big risk of fire.

And now: SIT DOWN for 15 minutes of concentration.

Do the same regular.

And then find yourself a teacher.

Master Horst is available if you live in the Bridport / Dorset area.

For online advice write to hdlindenau@hotmail.com

Suggested readings

Although the art of Jiu-Jitsu has to be mainly studied on the mat, in the dojo under supervision of a sensei and qualified martial arts instructor, I have to point out, that the theoretical approach to these studies are essential too. Therefore you always find the theory test in each grading syllabus and when it comes to Dan grades, a more elaborate assignment must be written by the brown belt candidate.

Sources for detailed background information are usually books. I have got myself only a hundred martial arts related books in my shelf. I give you some titles of my favorite books here.

Today it is very common to find further information online. But be aware, unless you are well trained in online research, you end up with the common stuff, which is often dictated by commerce and fashion.

Despite the fact, one can find all sorts of description in video form, any techniques, detailed, in slow motion, with subtitles and any style in performance, until today it is not possible to learn this art of Jiu-Jitsu online and/or from books only.

My recommendations are:

Zen in the martial arts / Joe Hyams / 1979 / ISBN 0-87477-101-3

Wu-Wei / Henri Borel / 1948 / Drei Eichen Verlag, Munich

Ki im taeglichen Leben / Koichi tohei / 1987 / ISBN 3 921508 14 2

Jiu-Jitsu - Lehrbuch fuer Selbstverteidung / Hans Reuter / 1923 / J.Gierl, Munich

Goshin-Jitsu no Kata / S. Addamiani /1986 / Weinmann / ISBN 3-87892-012-1

Vom Schueler zum Meister / Horst Weiland / 1993 / Brune Druck,

WHV

Martial Arts / J.Corcoran + E. Farkas / 1988 / USA, 08317-5805-8

…and by the way, if you find any mistake in this compendium – be aware I did it on purpose. Just for you, because there are always people they find the mistakes with others. But never with themselves.

Last but not least. I wrote this book in English and this is not my mother tongue. So please forgive me for any wrong spelling, it can only get better. I appreciate your comments and suggestions for a second edition. You can write to the author here in English or German.

Horst D. Lindenau

hdlindenau@hotmail.com

https://ichinenbridport.com/

Ichinen Bridport / UK

"MAY THIS HUMBLE COMPENDIUM GET IN THE RIGHT HANDS"

Master Horst D. Lindenau is a 2nd Dan in the art of traditional Jiu-Jitsu. He is born German and lives and teaches now in England. Since 1998 he is diploma sports teacher for martial arts and Yoga. His own schools have produced more than only black belts but changed many students life to the better. At the age of 65 he is still teaching in his local martial arts school named ICHINEN BRIDPORT. This club today is the follower of his former German schools SDS Bremen and Ichinen Bremen.

This book is for the student who wants to become a black belt in Jiu-Jitsu and Master Horst D. Lindenau offers lots of practical advice for assistance to reach this goal. You find detailed information about the art itself, some history and the author describes his own way with Jiu-Jitsu. A part of this book contains the Jiu-Jitsu syllabus from the beginner white belt up to the black belt as it is used for grading at Ichinen Bridport martial art school.

Jiu-Jitsu

ISBN: 9781521481042

You want to be a black belt and graduate as first Dan Jiu-Jitsu? You are right here to read what Master Horst D. Lindenau has to offer you. His own way with the martial arts will not only encourage you but gives you the practical advice you are looking for.

A martial artist for 40 years and former navy captain, Master Horst gives you detailed advice from all over the world and enables you to trigger your inner power and strength to become this black belt yourself.

Jiu-Jitsu is one of the oldest traditional Japanese arts of combat and in this compendium you find its challenges and secrets, its supremacy over other styles and gives you the necessary understandings.

"My way with Jiu-Jitsu" describes the path you have to conquer and gives you the practicable help to do so. The beginner will be guided through all aspects of Jiu-Jitsu and the advanced student will bring his own studies to the long aimed goal. This book describes the very own journey of a man, who has been involved into the martial arts from early childhood and travelled 68 countries to collect a wide knowledge of this fine art. The book supplies you with a daily routine schedule and a step by step syllabus to reach your own goal, to become a Jiu-Jitsu black belt.

Printed in Poland
by Amazon Fulfillment
Poland Sp. z o.o., Wrocław

50916188R00077